IPR HANDBOOK
FOR
PHARMA STUDENTS AND
RESEARCHERS

IPR HANDBOOK FOR PHARMA STUDENTS AND RESEARCHERS

By

Dr. Parikshit Bansal
Intellectual Property Management Dept.
National Institute of Pharmaceutical Education and Research
(NIPER) Mohali

PharmaMed Press
An imprint of Pharma Book Syndicate
An unit of **BSP Books Pvt., Ltd.**
4-4-309/316, Giriraj Lane,
Sultan Bazar, Hyderabad - 500 095.

Disclaimer

"Views expressed by the author in this book are his own and do not reflect the views of the institute or the organization to which he belongs"

Published by :

PharmaMed Press
An imprint of Pharma Book Syndicate

An unit of BSP Books Pvt., Ltd.

4-4-309/316, Giriraj Lane, Sultan Bazar, Hyderabad - 500 095.
Phone: 040-23445605, 23445688; Fax: 91+40-23445611
E-mail: info@pharmamedpress.com
www.pharmamedpress.com/pharmamedpress.net

ISBN : 978-93-5230-018-1 (HB)

ACKNOWLEDGEMENT

To

Dr. Naresh Kumar

For his affection, encouragement and guidance

Contents

About the Author

Dr.Parikshit Bansal is an IP educator and consultant. Currently working as an Asstt.Prof. (Intellectual Property Management) at the National Institute of Pharmaceutical Education and Research (NIPER) Mohali , he is also actively engaged in providing IPR and technology related consultancy to Industries under the consultancy program of the institute. He holds a Doctorate in Reproductive Biochemistry and has specialized in the area of male and female reproduction. As an overseas fellow, he worked at the Human IVF and reproduction lab at the Ottawa Civic Hospital, Ottawa, Canada and was also awarded the Canadian Govt. Commonwealth Fellowship..

An expert member with the All India Council of Technical Education (AICTE), New Delhi, Dr.Bansal is a nominated expert with the Arbitration and Mediation Centre of the World Intellectual Property Organization (WIPO), Switzerland. He worked as associate in WHO sponsored study, on " Impact of TRIPS on Pharmaceuticals, with specific reference to Generics in India" carried out by NIPER under the aegis of Ministry of Health and Family Welfare, Government of India.

Dr.Bansal is an active inventor and has filed nearly 12 patents relating to different inventions of his. He has been granted three patents, including one US patent. He has a deep practical experience of IPRs, especially patents and technology management, spanning more than a decade.

His lectures on IPRs have been widely appreciated by various organizations. Amongst selected organizations who have invited him for lectures are IIT, Delhi; GOA Pharmaceutical Manufacturers Association (GPMA), Goa; SSI, Solan; Panjab University, Chandigarh; National Instt. Of Technical Teachers' Training and Research (NITTTR), Chandigarh; Goa Institute of Management, Goa; Japan Institute of Invention and Innovation (JIII) , and Japanese Patent Office (JPO), Japan; European Union-Trade Investment Development Program, New Delhi; Indian Pharmaceutical Graduates Association (IPGA), New Delhi and Army Institute of Law, Mohali.

A few words for my readers

The word 'Kunji' means key. In India, 'Kunji' has an element of "naughtiness" associated with it. It denotes a guide or a 'small handbook' usually used by 'notorious' students who would be too busy 'bunking classes' to ready the normal 'heavy' textbooks. Written in a crisp manner, the 'kunji' surprisingly enabled such students to clear exams, which is all they wanted! The "Kunji" literally acted as a 'key' in opening up 'difficult subjects'!

The teaching of Intellectual Property Rights to science students poses a real challenge. There are many who consider IPRs to be the domain of law students and not science students. The subject is 'dry'- there are no wet-lab practicals! When I started teaching I wondered how to stimulate my students, excite them and open up the world of "IPRs" to them?

The concept of 'kunji' came to my rescue. I found they cover essentials of several topics 'under one roof', use easy language and fit into the syllabus. They don't take long to read. A similar 'kunji' or 'Handbook' in IPRs could hold the interest of students/researchers and make it easier for them to 'unlock' detailed books, already available. With this concept in mind, I wrote "IPR Handbook for Pharma Students and Researchers", to make the journey of pharma students/researchers into the world of IPRs simple, easy and enjoyable !

Why is there so much lack of understanding of IPRs? Maybe because the subject is yet to be introduced at graduate or post-graduate level, not only in India, but other countries too. Professionals e.g., engineers, chemists, doctors, researchers in different branches of science, all study their own subjects in detail but not IPRs. It is these very professionals who later join industries or rise to senior level positions involving policy level decisions. **Hence, introduction of the subject at student and research level during professional study/research, can be a powerful tool in promoting IPR understanding and acceptance, globally.**

Accordingly, a 'basic IPR syllabus' has been given by me at the end of this handbook, to help teachers not only in India, but elsewhere too who want to introduce the subject in regular teaching- preferably at undegraduate level. Positioning at UG level has sound logic- a researcher must have working knowledge of IPRs BEFORE he starts his research!

I sincerely hope that this 'kunji' gets tucked away in every bag and 'baggage' of students worldwide and used so much that its pages get stained and torn!

Dr.Parikshit Bansal

Chandigarh, India

August, 2007

How to use this book- the car analogy

People laugh when I ask them that is it necessary to be a mechanical engineer to drive a car. The answer, given with a smile is 'no'. The car is a very complicated piece of engineering. However, its success is ensured by the ability to be driven and used by common people, people who need not be engineers! Would it be possible for us to drive cars so easily and comfortably if we had to understand how the engine works, how the fuel is used, what functions the parts perform? No. We would be overawed and probably find it very difficult to drive cars. But we do drive cars. Why? Because we master the basics- the clutch, the steering and the brakes. We use cars to reach our destinations, we use them as vehicles for movement, without going into how they work. Whenever there is a problem, we go to the respective expert- the electrical man or the engine expert or just the gas station in case we run out of fuel.

Similar is the case of IPRs. You need not be a legal or IPR expert to use them practically. What you need to be is a technical professional, which you as a pharma student already are! Knowledge of IPRs can be a very powerful tool in helping you to improve the quality of your research, in helping to commercialize your research or even in finding new career avenues!

Just as in case of a car, whenever there is a problem you go to experts, so also in case of IPRs. Whenever you feel an area is difficult, or you need to file a patent or need guidance, you can freely consult experts. Problems do come when you buy a car, but that doesn't stop you from enjoying the pleasure of driving. Problems will come when you start learning about IPRs but that should not prevent you from experiencing the pleasure and thrill which the knowledge of IPRs will give to you, especially with regards to research.

Happy driving!

Summary of contents of each chapter

Chapter No. Title

1. What are IPRs?

In this chapter it is explained why the words 'intellectual' and 'property' are used when we talk about Intellectual Property. Also, why there are eight different types of IPRs and why one type is not possible. Features of each type are given in easy tabular form. A memory aid is given to help you to remember the essential features of IPR. A simple table is also included illustrating how IPRs are different from regulatory issues.

2. How are IPRs practically useful for pharma students and researchers?

In this chapter it is explained with help of illustrative stories, how pharma students can practically utilize the power and benefit of IPRs to improve the quality of their research work. Various factors affecting choice of IP protection are discussed.

3. How can I file a patent?

Filing a patent is a grey area for most researchers and students. In this chapter it is explained in a simple and easy manner, how a researcher can actually file a patent. Practical aspects of patenting e.g. forms, fee, precautions etc. are discussed .

In addition, tips on international patenting e.g. filing a patent in Europe or USA are also discussed. Recent amendments in the Indian Patent Act and its significance for Pharma Professionals are duly covered. Basic concepts of mailbox applications or WTO applications are introduced.

4. **How should I commercialize my patent?**

Filing a patent is important. But what is more important is to commercialize it! Patents filed, but not commercialized are a waste of precious human and financial resources. In this chapter, practical aspects of commercialization of patents are discussed. Concepts of Transfer of Technology (TOT) and Capture of Technology (COT) are introduced. Practical tips and suggestions are given for commercializing patents.

5. **How can I integrate IPRs into my research work?**

The knowledge of IPRs is not merely theoretical, but very applied and practical, provided one understands and makes use of it. In this chapter, a 'workable strategy' for integration of IPRs and technology management into research, by students and researchers is discussed.

6. **Why are ethics important in IPRs?**

The knowledge of IPRs is not merely theoretical, but very applied and practical. Owing to confidential nature of information being disclosed, it becomes imperative for IPR professionals to maintain a high standard of ethics and values, so that the trust reposed in them by inventors is not violated.

7. **What are the important IPR related treaties and international agreements I should be aware of as a Pharma student?**

In this chapter, important international treaties and agreements which a pharma professional should be aware of, are discussed and explained. GATT/TRIPS and WTO, DOHA declaration (including data exclusivity concepts) and HATCH-WAXMAN ACT.

8. **What are the career options for me in the area of IPRs?**

For a student, the first and foremost question regarding any new study area or subject is 'how useful will this be for me in getting a job?' As IPRs are yet to be introduced in professional colleges, but expectations of knowledge of IPRs is there during interviews, this handbook can be very useful. In this chapter, career options for pharma professionals in the area of IPRs are discussed. Job profiles and expected skill sets, apart from technical background are also discussed.

9. **How can I improve my qualifications in the area of IPRs?**

In this chapter, addresses of universities, list of IPR courses being offered, fee structure, qualifications etc. are provided so that students who want to work further in the area of IPRs can easily pursue these. Emphasis is given on distance learning courses, so that a student while pursuing his main degree is able to polish his skills in the area of IPRs also! Alternatively, for students who join industry and take up jobs, distance learning courses offer an excellent opportunity to acquire IPR knowledge and skills.

Annexure

How to use this Handbook as an IPR teaching manual for Pharma students?

An important aspect of this book is that owing to coverage of a very broad range of IPR concepts, it can be easily used as a 'teaching manual ' also. It represents a 'single window' source of information, thus facilitating lectures on IPRs by existing faculty. Introduction and teaching of IPRs, thus practically becomes easy.

Proposed syllabus and lecture coverage is included.

Suggestions for improvement are always welcome.
Feedback and suggestions can be emailed to the author at
pbansal.niper@gmail.com

CHAPTER-1

What are IPRs?

In this chapter it is explained why the words 'intellectual' and 'property' are used when we talk about Intellectual Property. Also, why there are eight different types of IPRs and why one type is not possible. Features of each type are given in easy tabular form. A memory aid is also given to help you to remember the essential features of IPR. A simple table is also included illustrating how IPRs are different from regulatory issues.

What are IPRs?

IPRs stands for "Intellectual Property Rights".

> "IPRs are LEGAL rights which are granted to a person for CREATIONS of the mind or intellect which have COMMERCIAL VALUE".

SINCE CREATIONS OF THE MIND DIFFER TOO MUCH e.g., the effort in composing a song or directing a movie is quite different from that in developing a new molecule for therapeutic use or an improved process for manufacturing a drug, it is not possible to have only one mechanism to protect all creations of the mind.

HENCE, THERE ARE EIGHT WELL-DEFINED MECHANISMS TO PROTECT CREATIONS OF THE MIND viz.

1. Patents
2. Copyright
3. Trademark
4. Industrial designs
5. Layout designs of integrated circuits
6. Geographical indications
7. Registration of plant varieties
8. Trade secrets.

Why the word property is used in case of 'intellectual property'?

The term 'Property' is normally associated with physical objects. On the other hand, there is no physical object, when one talks of Intellectual Property. Still the word 'property' is used. This is because just like any conventional property e.g., house, car, etc., intellectual property also has COMMERCIAL VALUE and can be BOUGHT AND SOLD. Hence, the word 'property' is used in case of intellectual property. However, intellectual property is different from conventional property in the sense that it is INTANGIBLE i.e., it can neither be seen nor felt.

Essential Features which define Property

Irrespective of nature and type of property i.e., whether it is conventional property e.g., car, house, consumer goods, material possessions etc., or intellectual property, there are certain essential features associated with property:

i) **Documentation:** Irrespective of its nature, commercial property always has some form of documentation associated with it e.g., Deed of Registration for land, Registration certificate for vehicle, Patent for Intellectual property or even a simple Cash Bill issued by owner of shop from which a consumer good is purchased etc.

ii) **Legally authorized government issuing agency:** Documentation regarding property is invariably issued by a legally recognized government agency e.g., Urban Development Authority in case of housing property, Licensing and Registering authority in case of Registration Certificate of a vehicle and the Controller of Patents in case of Patents. In case of consumer goods, obviously shopkeeper issuing a bill at first glance may not appear to be a legally authorized issuing agency. But the bill has certain registration numbers which are issued by appropriate legally authorized government agencies. Thus, indirectly, they control issue of the ownership certificate i.e., bill for purchase of consumer good e.g., TV, stereo etc.

iii) **Description:** Documentation regarding property ALWAYS carries a detailed description of the property which defines its location, features etc.

iv) **Ownership :** Name of persons/firms/establishments who own the property are always clearly mentioned in the document pertaining to that property.

v) **Time duration:** Ownership of property may or may not be be limited by a time frame e.g., in case of landed property, ownership is permanent. However, in case of registration of vehicles or even patents, there is a time validity period referred to as "Term of the Document" e.g., in case of patents, term of patent is twenty years.

vi) **Fee:** Property related documentation always involves some amount of expenditure e.g., registration fee, filing fee etc. Also, since the term is long, some sort of maintenance fee is levied on account of expenses for maintaining the set-up to provide necessary documentation.

vii) **Commercial value:** A defining feature of property is 'commercial value' owing to the fact that it can be bought and sold. If it cannot be sold, it cannot have commercial value.

MEMORY AID

Visualize the registration certificate (RC) of your mobike or car- it covers all features as discussed above

Why are intellectual property rights important?

The fundamental concept behind all forms of intellectual property rights is that THE PERSON WHO HAS PUT IN ORIGINAL EFFORT, MUST BE REWARDED. This is to encourage INNOVATION and CREATIVITY, so that society can prosper and progress.

If there was no mechanism to protect and reward original effort and creativity, eventually nobody would want to make any effort and society would be the loser!

Illustration:

- You put in lot of hard work and effort and come up with a very good invention. The moment you discuss it with someone, it is copied. You can neither prevent it nor get any credit for all your hard work. Will you be motivated to come up with new inventions?
- You spend years writing a laboratory manual. When it is ready, somebody just publishes it and takes all the profits. Will you be motivated to put in effort again?

Hence, it is very important that adequate legal mechanisms are in place to reward original thinkers and innovators and prevent unauthorized duplication.

Mechanisms for Intellectual Property Protection (IPP)

As discussed, there are eight mechanisms for protection of Intellectual Property as given below. Important features of each are discussed individually, in brief. Patents have been discussed in detail in other chapters, keeping in view their importance for pharma students and researchers. Web links for other mechanisms have been given to avoid too much text.

1. Patents 2.Industrial Designs 3. Layout Designs of Integrated Circuits
4.Copyrights 5. Trademarks 6. Geographical Indications (Gis)

7. Plant Breeder's Rights 8.Trade Secrets

1. Patents

Definition : "A patent is an exclusive right granted by the government to the original inventor/developer/researcher of an invention, which prohibits others from making, using or selling that invention."

Benefits

- The grant of exclusive rights encourages people to come up with new inventions and innovations for the benefit of society.
- The grant of a patent, apart from profitability is also associated with considerable peer respect and recognition which can be a strong motivating factor for many a researcher.

Precautions

A patent is granted after submission of an application fulfilling certain statutory/legal requirements, to the concerned patent office of a country. Patents are usually granted for a specified period only and must be kept 'alive' by payment of fee on regular basis, failing which they lapse and ownership rights granted to the owner come to an end.

Term

20 years

Registration

Patents in India are granted by the Controller of Patents, having Head Office at Calcutta and Branches at New Delhi, Madras and Mumbai (Annexure-1) .

Details at **www.patentoffice.nic.in**

2. Industrial Designs

> ***Definition:* "Industrial Designs refer to specific shape, configuration, surface, pattern or color or combination thereof which produces an aesthetic impression of the article."**

The important purpose of design Registration is to see that the artisan, creator, originator of a design having aesthetic look is not deprived of his bonafide reward by others applying it to their goods. Under WTO obligations, protection must be provided by the member countries, to new or original industrial designs. Member countries however have been given the option to exclude from protection, designs which are dictated by functional or technical consideration rather than aesthetics. It must be remembered that it is aesthetic considerations which constitute coverage of Industrial Designs e.g. the design of a ballpen, consisting of a particular color and body shape, or even the design of a particular bottle used for packaging a pharmaceutical product.

To make Indian Laws Compliant with WTO obligations in this respect, a new act, 'The Industrial Design Act, 2000' was enacted by Indian Parliament replacing the Designs Act, 1911. The act came into force w.e.f. 11.5.2001.

Benefits

- Prevents unauthorized copying of an original design. On account of better aesthetics , the design may lead to enhanced commercial value of a product.
- Protection period is sufficiently long- ten years and can be renewed for another five years by payment of fee.

Precautions

Ensure registration before disclosure in any form

Term

Maximum term is 15 years.

Registration

By making an application to Registrar of Designs, having Head Office at Kolkata (Annexure-1) .

Details at **www.patentoffice.nic.in**

3. Layout Designs of Integrated Circuits

> ***Definition: "Layout designs for integrated circuits refer to the specific manner in which transistors and other circuitry elements of an integrated circuit (IC) are laid out in a semiconductor IC and includes lead wires connecting such elements."***

Semiconductor IC is a product having transistors and other circuitry elements, which are inseparably formed on a semi-conductor material or an insulating material or inside the semiconductor material and designed to perform an electronic circuitry function.

The Act for protection of the layout designs of Integrated Circuits came into force on 4th September, 2000 and is called the SICLD (Semiconductor Integrated Circuit Layout Design) Act, 2000. The Act provides for exclusive rights to the registered proprietor of a layout design and also to the registered users. Applications for registration of layout designs must be filed with the Registrar. Appeals against the orders of the Registrar could be filed with the Appellate Board. The Act also provides for criminal prosecution for infringement of layout designs. The administration department for implementation of the Act in India is Department of information Technology, Ministry of Communications and Information Technology, Government of India.

Benefits

- ♣ Protection of effort and investments in design and improvement of circuits
- ♣ Recognition of original effort

Precautions

- Term of registration also includes period during which design is not commercially exploited e.g. a design not exploited commercially for more than 2 years from date of registration of application shall be treated as commercially exploited for the purpose of the act.
- Know what is registrable and what is not because not all circuit designs can be registered. Layout designs which are :
  i) Not original or already commercially exploited
  ii) Not distinctive
  iii) Not capable of being distinguishable from any other regis tered layout design
  are not registrable.

Term

10 years from date of filing or known date of commercialization , whichever is earlier.

Registration

By maing an application to Registrar, SICLDL New Delhi, India (Annexure1).

Weblinks

FAQ on Semiconductor Act **http://www.mit.gov.in/act/faqsc.asp**

Semiconductor Integrated Circuits Layout-Design Registry (SICLDR) **http://www.mit.gov.in/sicldr.asp**

The Semiconductor Integrated Circuits Layout Design Act 2000 **http://www.mit.gov.in/semiconductorAct.pdf**

The Semiconductor Integrated Circuits Layout Design Rules 2001 **http://www.mit.gov.in/srules/nsbill.asp**

4. Copyrights

Definition: "Copyrights are a set of exclusive rights granted by law to the creators and producers of forms of creative expressions such as literary, musical and cinematographic works."

The best forms of copyrights are authored and edited books, or audio and video cassettes, which cannot be reproduced without the permission of the person (author, editor or publisher) who holds the copyright. In case of Patents and trade secrets, protection of the basic idea is granted but in case of copyright, protection is possible only on the expressed material (printed, painted, tape recorded, video recorded or expressed in any other form e.g. computer software).

Copyright has got only limited protection because though one may not photocopy a book or make a copy of a audio or video tape or a CD, one can still use the ideas/knowledge given in them for any purpose. However, this is not so in case of patents and trade secrets. An instruction manual can be protected by copyright and also protected as a trade secret (if developed by a company only for internal use), but it cannot be patented.

Benefits

- Confers protection from copying to a piece of work which is neither patentable nor can be kept as a trade secret
- Imparts commercial value to a work
- Ensures rewards in form of recognition
- Financial benefits in terms of royalty payments, which can be transferred to legal heirs also, depending upon terms and conditions of licensing

Precautions

- Due application must be made to registrar of copyrights, before any attempt at commercialization/licensing/permission
- Copyright rules may be modified from time to time as has been done to allow protection rights in case of computer software. Update yourself.
- Be aware of the loopholes. In biotechnology, copyright may cover DNA sequence data which may be published. However, introduction of a wobble sequence in the same genetic code for same protein will allow publication of an alternative genetic code without infringing copyright.
- Know what is covered and what is not. Computer databases and photomicrographs of DNA instruction manuals related to Biotechnology can also be covered under copyright protection.

Term

Entire lifetime of an author and 50 years after his death.

Registration

Copyright protection in India is obtained from Registrar of Copyrights, New Delhi (Annexure-1) . Details at **http:// copyright.gov.in**

5. Trademarks

> *Definition: "A trademark is a word or a symbol adopted and used by a manufacturer or a merchant to identify his goods and distinguish them from those manufactured or sold by others."*

In biotechnology research, certain vectors useful in recombinant research are known by their trade names. Certain laboratory equipments and devices used by workers in labs may also bear trademarks. Nearly all pharmaceutical products bear a distinctive trademark, which identifies the company making/marketing it.

Benefits:

- Trademarks are a vital and quickly recognized symbol of a corporation and its products and services.
- They have a lot of goodwill associated with them, which enhances market value of products bearing that trademark.
- Basic purpose is to identify goods as belonging to a particular manufacturer so that he gets the benefit of maintaining a particular level of excellence.
- Hence, trademarks have significant commercial value and must be protected and defended, throughout local markets or those parts of the world where the company or product may be recognized or found.

Precautions:

- Use of a trademark must be proper in the sense that it must be used as an adjective followed by the noun describing the product e.g. Xerox Photostat machine.

- The improper use of a trademark can result in its loss as an exclusive proprietary term e.g., aspirin was once the trademark of Bayer; Xerox had to spend lot of money to educate consumers that Xerox is its trademark and the term Xerox should not be used in place of Photostat.
- The improper use of a trademark as a noun encourages the public to perceive the trademark as the generic name of the product and not as a protectable brand name e.g., Xeroxing, Dalda
- The duration of a trademark and other such intellectual property matters vary from country to country. There is no central world body for trademarks, so they must be registered on a country-by-country basis.

Term

Initial registration is for a period of 10 years, but can be renewed indefinitely.

Registration

Trademarks registration in India is governed by the Trade Marks Registry having its head office at Mumbai (Annexure-1) .

Details at **www.patentoffice.nic.in**

6. Geographical Indications

Definition: " Geographical indications of Goods are defined as that aspect of Intellectual Property which relate to goods or products originating from a particular geographical region situated in a particular country"

They are used to identify only three categories of goods - agricultural, natural or manufactured. The manufactured goods should be produced or processed or prepared in that territory and must have a special quality or reputation. Typically, such a name conveys an assurance of quality and distinctiveness which is essentially attributable to the fact of its origin in that defined geographical locality, region or country e.g. Darjeeling Tea, Nagpur oranges, Bikaneri Bhujiya (an Indian snack resembling stiff salted noodles) Agra Petha, Mathura Peda (Indian sweets), Basmati rice and so on.

Geographical Indications are covered as an element of IPRs under Articles 1 (2) and 10 of the Paris Convention for the Protection of Industrial Property. They are also covered under Articles 22 to 24 of the agreement on Trade Related aspects of Intellectual Property Rights (TRIPS) , which was part of the Agreements concluding the Uruguay Round of GATT negotiations. India, as a member of the World Trade Organization (WTO), enacted the Geographical Indications of Goods (Registration & Protection)Act, 1999 which came into force w.e.f. 15th September 2003.

Benefits

♣ It confers legal protection to goods produced in a particular region.

♣ Enhances commercial value and increases market visibility for the produce

- Prevents unauthorised use of a Registered Geographical Indication by others
- Boosts exports by providing legal protection to goods covered under Geographical Indications
- Promotes economic prosperity of producers of goods from a particular geographical territory.

Precautions

- Applicable only to goods which are agricultural, natural or manufactured in a specific territory
- Specific only for goods from a particular geographical region which is registered as a GI.
- Can be obtained ONLY by registered bodies e.g. societies, associations etc. duly recognized by the law and not by individuals. Applicant MUST represent interest of the producers
- Registration is NOT one time and regular fee has to be paid to keep the registration valid.
- Registration cannot be licensed but can be transferred to successors, if original person dies

Term

One time registration is valid for ten years.

Registration

Registration of GI in India can be made by a duly recognized body by making an application in writing to Registrar of Geographical Indications, alongwith prescribed fee. (Annexure-1)

Details at **www.patentoffice.nic.in**

7. Plant Breeder's Rights

Definition: " These are legal rights granted by the govt. for protection of plant varieties, rights of farmers and plant breeders"

In most of the industrialized and developed countries, crop varieties can be protected as IP since certain rights are granted to the persons producing them. These rights are called 'Plant Breeder's Rights'. However, the present IPR systems were not designed to promote the protection of diversity of whole ecosystems or unmodified plants. Still, inventors do not lose the benefit of honest effort e.g. in identifying medicinal value of plant extract, since the evaluation, use and maintenance of plants is encouraged indirectly by the patent system.

The issue of protecting farmers' rights and also Plant Varieties became important once India signed the agreement on Trade Related aspects of Intellectual Property Rights (TRIPS) on 30th Dec.1994, which came into force on 1st January, 2005 after the expiry of a transition period of ten years . TRIPS seeks to promote effective promotion of IPR, giving members the freedom to determine appropriate method of implementing the provisions of the agreement with their own legal system and practise.Under article 27 of TRIPS , members must provide protection to plant varieties either by patenting or by an effective "sui generis" system (unique, that which cannot be classified with others) or by combination of both.

Protection of the above in India is covered under the Plant Varieties and Farmers' Rights Bill, 1999 which got status of Act in 2001 (The Protection of Plant Varieties and Farmers' Rights Act, 2001). It safeguards interests of the farmers and respects the traditional right of the farmer to save, use, share or sell his farm produce.

Benefits

- Promotion of biodiversity- If scope of PBR is broadened, it might help in extending breeding work to more crops, which in turn will promote greater biodiversity
- By assuring finacial return on new varieties developed, better and mission oriented research is encouraged.
- Indian researchers developed good varieties of plants but in absence of rights, these were freely available to all. New varieties developed as a result of these efforts got protected in other countries but not in India. PBR helps avoid such situations.
- Easy availability of good quality seeds developed internationally- In absence of protection, foreign companies were hesitant to release their improved seeds/varieties in India for fear of piracy. But if rights are available, this fear is removed.

Precaution

- Registration is forfeited if annual fee is not paid

Term

Period of protection quite long- 15 years for annual crops and 18 years for trees and vines. One time renewal at the end of 6 years in case of annual crops and 9 years in case of trees and vines on payment of prescribed fees

Registration

Registration of PV in India can be made by a duly recognized body by making an application in writing to Registrar of Plant Varieties, alongwith prescribed fee (Annexure-1).

Applications for plant varieties should be filed with the Authority. Department of Agriculture and Cooperation, Ministry of Agriculture, Government of India is the administrative department for implementation of this Act.

Weblinks:

Department of Agriculture and Cooperation, Ministry of Agriculture
http://agricoop.nic.in/

The Protection of Plant Varieties and Farmers' Rights Act 2001
http://agricoop.nic.in/PPV&FR%20Act,%202001.pdf

8. Trade Secret

Definition: " Trade secrets refer to proprietary information having commercial application and value."

A classic example of a trade secret is the formula for the soft drink, 'Coca- Cola' which has been preserved as a family secret, passed from one generation to another. It is true that specific information may have value but how to protect it as a trade secret? How to ensure that your employee does not cheat you by taking away information which you may have generated after years of hard work? Some of the highest selling products in pharmaceutical area, especially which are based on microbial technologies are protected as trade secrets or undisclosed information. It is quite often in the interest of the organization to keep some developments as a secret and trade it to gain commercial advantage.

Benenfits

- Minimal documentation
- No fee
- No expiry
- Monoply for almost unlimited period
- No territorial limits

Precautions

- Ensure adequate protection through legal measures. Do not be careless in communication in writing, oral or otherwise.
- Ensure back-up by proper documentation. Death/disease resulting in memory can result in loss of technology, unless it is

documented and kept in a safe place or shared with a trustworthy person.

Registration

India at present does not have any law to protect undisclosed information. However, WTO regulations require member countries to protect trade secrets. The WTO obligations require that proprietary information be protected to prevent others from using it without the consent of the owner, in a manner which is contrary to honest commercial practise. In India though no exclusive legislation exists but the matter would be generally covered under the Contract Act, 1872. The common law on the subject is constantly evolving and courts have provided relief where allegations of wrongful disclosure have been proven. A common tool used in the protection of trade secrets is NDA (Non-disclosure agreement) or a CDA (Confidentiality Agreement). Students seeking jobs after completion of their studies are likely to encounter these terms and may be asked to sign such documents by the companies where they are joining. These documents are all the more important in case of knowledge driven industries e.g. pharma/biotechnology and serve to prevent unauthorized disclosure of information, which can be damaging for an employer.

Table 1.1 IP mechanisms- Important Features.

IP Mechanism	Time of Protection	Jurisdiction	Fee	Authority/Agency concerned
1. **Patents**	20 years	National.	Rs.1000/- for Individuals and Rs.4000/- for corporates	Patent Office, India . Respective branches at Delhi, Calcutta, Bombay and Madras.
2. **Copyright**	During entire lifetime of author and 50 years after his death.	International, under the Berne Convention	Rs.50/- for literary, dramatic, musical or artistic work.	Registrar of Copyright, New Delhi
3. **Trademarks**	Initial protection period is 10 years but can be renewed indefinately	National.	Rs.2500/-	Registry of Trademarks, Bombay (HO), Calcutta
4. **Industrial Designs**	Initial 10 years, extendable to a maximum of 5 years. Thus, maximum term is 15 years.	National. Separate applications needed in different countries. Hague agreement facilitates.	Rs.1000/-	Designs can be registered at any of the respective Patent Offices at New Delhi, Mumbai, Calcutta or Madras
5. **Layout Designs of Integrated Circuits**	10 years.	National	-n.a.-	-n.a.-
6. **Plant Varieties**	15 years, annual crops 18 years for trees and vines.	National	Individual- Rs.5,000/- Educational- Rs.7000/- Commercial- Rs.10,000/-	Registrar of Plant Varieties, New Delhi
7. **Geographical Indications**	One time registration, valid 10 years. Renewal	National	-n.a.-	IP India offices at New Delhi, Calcutta, Bombay, Chennai. Main at Chenai.
8. **Trade Secrets**	No registration	National. Under law of natural justice	-	Civil courts

IPRs Vs Regulatory Issues

A few common question in the minds of students are " Are IPRs and Regulatory issues one and the same thing? Or are they different? What are the similarities and differences between the two?"

A clear understanding of both can help students in proper choice of careers. The emergence of the World Trade Organization (WTO) and the signing of Agreement on Trade Related Aspects of Intellectual Property Rights (TRIPS) made the industry realize that without adequate knowledge and focus on these areas, becoming a global player is next to impossible! Hence, for students and researchers it is important from a career perspective to clearly understand the links and differences between IPRs and Regulatory Issues.

> **IPRs** : "Intellectual Property Rights are legal rights associated with property which is of intellectual nature i.e. thoughts and ideas."

Nature

IPRs are rights associated with property which is intangible i.e. cannot be seen or felt , but has commercial value. They are not compulsory i.e. an individual/organization may or may not go for IPRs. Depending upon the nature of Intellectual Property, there are eight different mechanisms to protect it viz. Patents, Copyrights, Trademarks, Geographical Indications, Industrial Designs, Layout Designs of Integrated Circuits, Trade Secrets and Plant Breeder's Rights.

Significance

IPRs prevent commercial loss to individuals/organizations. By providing mechanisms to protect thoughts and ideas (or creations of the mind) having commercial value, IPRs prevent commercial loss e.g., to develop a process, lot of intellectual inputs e.g., research etc. might be involved. However, once it is developed and standardized, it can be easily copied. This would cause a loss to the person/organization who has originally invested time and money. Similarly, in case of an author who has written a book or artist who has sung a song , IPRs ensure protection by prohibiting unauthorized use and thus reward original effort.

Regulatory issues: "These are legal regulations associated with manufacturing and which are enforced by the government to ensure the safety and quality of pharmaceutical products".

Nature

Unlike IPRs which are voluntary in nature, Regulatory Issues are laws which have to be obeyed and complied with. They remain in force as long as a product is being manufactured and primary aim is public benefit i.e., ensuring safety and quality of the products being manufactured.

Significance

Regulatory issues ensure safety and quality of pharmaceutical products by providing guidelines to manufacturers.

Thus, the focus of both is entirely different ie. while IPRs focus on encouraging innovations and new developments, Regulatory Issues deal primarily with ensuring safety and quality of pharmaceutical products. Though there are certain similarities, the differences between the two areas are considerable. A proper understanding of the two can help students and researchers grasp the individual importance of each area and enable proper choice of careers and job profiles.

Table 2 IPRs vs Regulatory

Parameter	IPRs	Regulatory Issues
Similarities		
1. Status	Legally enforceable	Legally enforceable
2. Controls	Government	Government
3. Financial Implications	Fee involved	Fee involved
4. Purpose	Safeguard Public interest by rewarding original work and thus encouraging innovations.	Safeguard Public interest by ensuring quality and safety of pharmaceutical products.
5. Global status	Consensus on common filing procedures at regional/international level, but national rules governing grant of IPRs vary from country to country.	Consensus on standards which have to be met but otherwise vary greatly from country to country. International Conference on Harmonization (USA/ EU/ Japan)
6. Global applicability	Restricted to national level. Mechanisms for international protection still involve going through national route of each country. Regional protection mechanisms still developing.	Restricted to national level. Licenses granted in a particular country are applicable only in that country. Regional protection mechanisms still developing.
7. Effect on Trade	Regarded as barriers to international trade, since patented products cannot be copied	Regarded as barriers to international trade, since drugs being manufactured in one country may not be allowed to be sold/manufactured in other countries, unless regulatory requirements have been met.

Table 2 *Contd...*

Parameter	IPRs	Regulatory Issues
Differences		
1. Nature	Intellectual Property is of 8 different types and there are 8 different mechanisms to protect it viz. Patents, Trademarks, Copyrights, Industrial Designs, Layout Designs of Integrated Circuits, Geographical Indications, Plant Breeder's Rights and Trade Secrets. IPRs primarily ensure that original creator is rewarded. They have nothing to do with ensuring quality or safety of pharmaceutical products.	These are primarily rules and regulations (mechanisms) for ensuring **quality and safety** of pharmaceutical products. Regulatory issues have nothing to do with rewarding the innovators or inventors
2. Target segment	Original thinkers / innovators. Recognize, protect and reward original work.	Industry. Ensure that the products, which are manufactured and made available to public, meet certain standards of quality and safety.
3. Enforcement	Office of Controller of Patents, under the Ministry of Industry. No involvement of Ministry of Health or Environment.	**1.** Drug Controller General under Ministry of Health **2.** Environment Ministry for Pollution control aspects
4. Working	IPRs e.g. patents can be licensed out by institutes or can be used by Industry to protect their innovations.	Regulatory issues are worked (executed) through grants of permissions/ licenses mainly to industry.

Table 2 *Contd...*

Parameter	IPRs	Regulatory Issues
Differences		
5. Stage of application	IPRs come into force before commercialization and remain in force irrespective of whether product is commercialized or not. They have no direct link with manufacturing activity.	Regulatory issues are **only** for products which are commercialized. They are directly linked to manufacturing activity. If there is no manufacturing activity, there are no regulatory issues involved.
6. Binding	No. They are voluntary in nature. A person may or may not seek IPRs.	Compulsory. Regulatory issues offer no choice- they have to be complied with. However, degree of regulations vary depending on the rote taken for commercializing your product e.g. generic versus New Drugs.
7. Time period	After expiry of protection term, IPRs come into public domain to be freely used by all e.g. when patents of drugs expire, they come into public domain, permitting manufacture by others, as generic drugs.	Regulatory issues never expire. As long as manufacturing is going on, quality standards have to be maintained.
8. Stages	Starts from the time anything new originates in mind e.g. in form of design, painting, musical composition, literary work, invention etc. In case of inventions, steps involved for seeking patents are confirming novelty, non-obviousness and industrial application. Thereafter, replying to objections of the examiners and finally grant of patent.	Starts from the time molecule is tested for the first time in humans after completing animal trials. Trials in human are conducted in three phases- I, II and III and data generated forms part of the Investigational New Drug Application (INDA), NDA (New Drug Application), ANDA (Abbreviated New Drug Application) etc.

Table 2 *Contd...*

Parameter	IPRs	Regulatory Issues
Differences		
9. Inputs for multi-nation filing	More or less similar. A patent application filed in India for an invention, will involve only minor changes in format, language, presentation etc. when filed abroad. No new data requirements have to be met.	Inputs in terms of quality and quantity of data may vary considerably from one country to another. Fresh data may have to be generated to comply with regulatory requirements of a country.
10. Personnel involved for enforcement	Examiners / infringement lawyers / civil courts	Drugs controllers / drug inspector / govt. analysts
11. Legal status	Debatable and can be challenged. Subject to cancellation by courts.	Laws / beyond debate. Must be complied with by all.
12. Technology Contribution	IPRs particularly those related to inventions ie.patents, fuel innovations and new developments. They contribute to technology growth by resulting in documentation and dissemination of latest technologies vide patent databases. Also, they help prevent duplication of work.	No role in technology growth. Rather emphasis is on ensuring safety of products being manufactured using new technologies/ processes/ developments.
13. Role in business profitability	Play a key role in influencing business profitability by helping in identification of new technologies, worldwide technology trends, global players, preventing duplication of work and also encouraging development of new processes. Lead to revenue generation by licensing out	They are a part and parcel of business activities. No role in promoting profitability. Rather, they are regarded as hindrances and barriers to trade, which affect business profitability

Annexure - 1

List of Addresses :

Patents

Kolkata Branch Asst. Controller of Patents & Designs, Nizam Palace, 2nd MSO Building (5th to 7th Floors) 234/4 Acharya Jagadish Bose Road, Kolkata 700 020 Phone: 91-33-247 4401-03, 91-33-247 3851, 91-22-240 1353, Fax : 91-33-247 3851	**Delhi Branch** Asstt. Controller of Patents & Designs, Patent Office Branch Plot no. 32, Sector 14 Dwarka, New Delhi
Mumbai Branch Assistant Controller of Patents & Designs, Todi Estates, 3rd Floor, Sun Mill Compound, Lower Parel(West) Mumbai 400 013 Phone: 91-22-492 5092, 91-22-492 4058, Fax : 91-22-495 0622	**Chennai Branch** Assistant Controller of Patents & Designs Wing 'C' (C-4, A), III Floor, Rajaji Bhavan Besant Nagar, Chennai 600 090 India Phone: 91-44-490 1495, 91-44-490 1496, Fax : 91-44-490 1492
Industrial Designs Office of the Controller General of Patents, Designs and Trademarks The Trade Marks Registry, Old CGO Building 101, Maharshi Karve Road, Mumbai-400 020 Phone: 022-205 3372 Email : cgpdtmum@vsnl.net	**Copyright** The Registrar of Copyrights Copyright Office B-2/W-3, Curzon Road Barracks Kasturba Gandhi Marg, New Delhi-110 001 Phone: 011- 3384387 Fax: 011- 3384687
Trade Marks Registry (Head Office) Mumbai Central Building, M.Karve Road Mumbai-400 020 Phone- 022- 2017368, 286 4125, 2013700 Fax- 022-2013694 Email- tmrmum@bom5.vsnl.net.in	**Trade Marks Registry , KOLKATA** 1st Floor, 15/1, Chowringhee Square Kolkata-700069 Ph: 033-2480050, 2482840, 2434821 Fax: 033-248 2738 Email: tmrcalbr@wb.nic.in trmcalbr@cal2.vsnl.net.in

Registrar of Geographical Indication

The Registrar of Geographical Indication,
Guna complex, No.443/304 Anna Salai,
Teynampet, **Chennai-6000 018**
Phone: 044-4314293/94/95/96/97/98
Fax: 044-4314291
Email : girindia@vsnl.net

Registrar of Plant Varieties

Registrar, Protection of Plant Varieties and Farmers Rights Authority
New Delhi

CHAPTER-2

How are IPRs practically useful for pharma students and researchers?

In this chapter it is explained with help of illustrative stories, how pharma students and researchers can practically utilize the power and benefit of IPRs to improve the quality of their research work. Various factors affecting choice of IP protection are discussed alongwith role of IPRs in promoting business profits.

2. How are IPRs practically useful for pharma students and researchers?

Knowledge of IPRs especially patents can be very useful for pharma researchers, whether at Post-graduate or Ph.D level. Apart from researchers, IPRs are also very important for the industry, business managers and also economic growth and development of a country. For pharma researchers, it is important to understand how IPRs are interlinked. Overall importance of IPRs is discussed below alongwith illustrative stories, which are hypothetical but quite close to real life situations which researchers might encounter.

Significance of IPRs for Researchers

1. Prevent duplication of work

Search of patent databases reveals what has already been done before, thus saving precious time and money. Quite often, industry may just file a patent for an innovation and not publish it. On the other hand, a researcher/student not aware of IPRs may base his review of information purely on journal or literature only, thus missing key information.

Illustrative story - Vinatin's Ph.D project failure

Vinatin was doing his M.Pharm in a leading research institute. His guide was a renowned authority, working in the area of probiotic formulations. When Vinatin started his Ph.D. work, he carried out a thorough survey of literature. He was also given copies of the thesis of his seniors, conference proceedings and books which his guide was having. Vinatin and his guide carefully reviewed the literature and planned the research work. Over a period of four years, Vinatin worked day and night, carrying out experiments and generating data. Finally, the work was completed. During the course of interaction with a manufacturer in a conference, interest got generated in the project. The manufacturer visited Vinatin's lab and interacted with his guide. He evinced keen interest in the technology. However, prior to any committment, he forwarded details of the work to his R&D team. When he got back, he had very disappointing news for Vinatin and his guide. The work which they had carried out had been patented almost ten years ago by a European company. He provided a copy of the patent to Vinatin and his Guide. They were shocked to find that a large chunk of data which they had generated over a period of nearly four years, was already disclosed in the patent! They had unknowingly duplicated work which had already been patented several years before Vinatin started his work! The industry backed out from using Vinatin's work.

Analysis: *Neither Vinatin nor his guide were at fault-both had work honestly and sincerely. But in the end, their lack of knowledge of IPRs led to all their time, effort and money going waste. Not many students or guides search patent databases when planning their research projects, forgetting that the ultimate buyers of their work i.e. industry, will not publish papers but file patents! This leads to duplication of work, which can be easily avoided as above story shows. Had Vinatin carried out a search of the patent databases, he would have redesigned his experiments and carried out fresh research, which could have been utilized by industry, for benefit of society.*

Thus, PREVENTING DUPLICATION of work is a very important aspect of IPRs.

2. Help researchers to focus on commercially relevant research

Patents are for work having commercial value. For researchers formulating research projects, a review of patent databases quickly reveals what is 'hot' and what is not!

Illustrative Story - How Minawa's research project became an Industry favourite

Minawa and Remetti were two M.Pharma students working in the area of Natural Products in a leading research institute. Minawa had done a course on IPRs conducted by WIPO and had some basic knowledge of IPRs. Remetti on other hand had absolutely no knowledge of IPRs. When they started their research work, both got very good labs and guides. There was no problem of funds. The labs in case of both researchers were very well-equipped. Minawa interacted with his guide and requested permission to suggest a research project. He carried out a thorough search of patent databases in addition to literature and then proposed a research project. Remetti also designed a research project, but based on work being carried out already in the lab and as suggested by his seniors. Subsequently, both submitted their thesis and appeared for placements. Minawa easily got placement with a leading company and also had four offers from other companies. Remetti found it very difficult to get placements. Both had worked under identical conditions, worked hard, honestly. What happened?

Analysis: *It is true that both Minawa and Remetti worked in good labs and had access to good infrastructure. The only difference lay in research problem identification. Minawa selected a topic of 'hot' commercial relevance, based on information obtained by search of the patent databases. He found out that a particular ingredient obtained from a natural product having considerable therapeutic application, was being obtained at very low yields at industry level. This was leading to high prices of the formulations. He chose a project aimed at carrying out screening of various varieties of the natural sources to identify a 'high concentration' variety and also standardizing a process for its extraction. Based on knowledge of* *existing processes as given in literature and patents, Minawa tried out some innovative approaches and developed a novel and simple process for which he filed a patent and then published it. He also informed a few industries (address obtained from patents) about his work. Naturally, his work generated lot of interest! He had solved an industry problem, carried out work which had immediate application. The result was very good offers from industry. In contrast, Remetti chose a work which resulted in good publication but had no immediate industrial significance. During interviews, he had to compete with several other candidates who had similar profiles. This made the competition tough. In contrast, Minawa's work stood out. The only thing which made a difference was a basic knowledge of IPRs and its integration with ongoing research work.*

Thus, IPRs play a key role in identification of 'hot' areas of research. This enables researchers to utilize existing facilities and short research periods, to conduct work of high impact value- not only in terms of publication, but also actual usage by industry.

3. Prevent exploitation of workers

By enabling researchers to have 'legal rights' over their work, IPRs prevent exploitation of workers and ensure proper remuneration, in case their work is used for commercial purposes

Illustrative story - Viminka and her lost million dollars

Viminka was working as a researcher in a govt. funded research project related to reproductive biology. During the course of her work, she came across a peculiar problem of non-reproducibility of sperm counts in specific cases, when using existing method of staining and counting as given by a manufacturer of an automated instrument. She tried to overcome the same and was successful. She discussed the process with her supervisor. He called the manufacturer for discussions. The process was discussed in detail with the manufacturer, who appreciated Viminka's work. However, when the matter of transfer of rights and financial payments was discussed, practical problems arose. The laboratory had no legal 'rights' over the work. They had not filed a patent nor signed any confidentiality agreement (CDA) /non-disclosure agreement (NDA) with manufacturer while discussing their project. Viminka's work was used by the manufacturer, with neither public recognition nor any financial gains for her. She ended up getting exploited in absence of protection.

Analysis: *Viminka's initiative and hard work went unrewarded because of a very simple lapse on her part. She should have generated rights over her 'inventive process' by filing a patent for her work or at least signing a NDA/CDA with manufacturer thus protecting her work as a trade secret. In absence of a patent or CDA, no rights were created and manufacturer was able to use Viminka's work, free of cost.*

Thus, generation of legal rights over one's work and preventing exploitation of researchers is a very important aspect of IPRs.

4. Help in revenue generation

Licensing of patents helps to earn money – for researchers and also the institute and departments. This in turn leads to financial freedom-better research facilities, improved infrastructure.

Illustrative story - How Paritiken got a ten-year scholarship

Paritiken, a Ph.D scholar while working on the bench encountered practical problems in carrying out purification of his protein samples. He tinkered around and developed an improved column for carrying out chromatography of his samples. The rugged performance, ease of use and simplicity of his 'innovation' was appreciated by his supervisor who suggested further modifications. Eventually, Paritiken was able to design an improved column for chromatography, which was significantly better than existing columns. A patent was filed for the same. Paritiken then interacted with the representatives of companies who were visiting his lab, showed them the column and conveyed that patent for the same had been filed. The invention generated a lot of interest. He recieved rapid offers from two leading companies working in the area. Subsequently, one of the companies was able to secure the rights, after paying a handsome amount to the institute as downpayment. In addition, a royalty amount was also agreed upon for ten years. Paritiken as the inventor, not only got a significant share of the downpayment, but he also got a 'scholarship' for ten years in terms of 'royalty' payments for his invention!!

The money generated through his invention also helped the department in procuring an advanced HPLC machine, which had been pending for a long time due to shortage of funds.

Analysis: *A simple effort i.e. filing of a patent resulted in a 'win-win' situation for all- the researcher, his department, the industry and also other researchers who were able to get access to a new product.*

5. Important source of technical information

Patents are the ONLY source regarding detailed technical information, which is unlikely to be available anywhere else. While number of journals may be in hundreds, the patent database per country is only one, making consultation much easier.

Illustrative story - How Wami manufactured his own reagents

Wami, a post-graduate student required large quantities of TMB, a substrate for the enzyme horse radish peroxidase, which he was using in his research work. When he checked up with the supplier, he got a shock- the reagent was in short supply and the costing was too high for his limited research budget. He discussed the matter with his friend Minawa, who advised him to search for details on the internet, by browsing patent databases. With the help of Minawa, Wami was able to locate a patent in which full details of preparing TMB were given. Using the details provided, Wami was very easily able to prepare sufficient quantities of the reagent for his research work. Also, the costing fitted very well within his laboratory budget.

Analysis: *Knowledge of IPRs is important not only in preventing duplication, securing rights, preventing exploitation and helping in revenue generation. It can also be helpful for researchers in overcoming 'sticky' problems of limited funds, as the above story illustrates.*

6. Prevent infringements and help avoid litigation

A basic knowledge of IPRs enables researchers to respect others rights and decide whether their work is infringing or not, especially in commercial segment.

Illustrative story - How Tinamara comercialized his work

Tinamara, a Post-doc fellow developed a new process for a biocatalyst being employed extensively in the pharma industry. He got in touch with the industry and discussed the possibility of transferring his work to them. Industry asked him to confirm whether his work was truly novel or was infringing upon somebody's else's patent. On checking, Tinamara found that though his process was novel, certain aspects of the work were anticipated by two earlier patents. He discussed the matter with his patent attorney, who told him that in event of use of his process by the industry, possibility of litigation could not be avoided. However, the attorney advised

Tinamara not to get discouraged and see whether he could modify the process and make it non-infringing. Tinamara tried and was successful in developing a non-infringing process. He got the same confirmed from the attorney and then successfully transferred it to the industry.

Analysis: *"Prevention is better than cure" as the adage goes. Tinamara, due to his knowledge of IPRs was able to give a robust process to the industry, in which any doubts or threats of litigation had been completely eliminated.*

7. Stimulate creativity

By enabling researchers to see at a glance the level of technological achievement in a particular field, patents stimulate creativity. They impose challenges for researchers as to how to take their achievements even further.

Illustrative story - Wirami and the new culture media

Wirami, an M.Pharm student was trying to develop a media for culturing a particular strain of microbes isolated in his lab earlier. The existing commercially available media was too costly and the ones he tried to come up with were already patented. Not wanting to give up, Wirami kept trying and one day accidentally tried an unusual combination, utilizing bio-waste. To his surprise and joy, he obtained unprecedented growth in all his cultures.

Analysis: *Patents, rather than acting as barriers, had 'fuelled' his innovation and creativity, resulting in a low-cost technology.*

8. Help in identification of career opportunities

At doctoral level, one tends to work in a super-specialized area. Finding matching employers, who can possibly enable opportunities in a similar area becomes a chance factor or a rare possibility.

However, knowledge of IPRs can help in the easy and accurate location of industries working in a specific area, thus helping to strengthen career opportunities of researchers.

Illustrative story - How Vibristika found the company she could not find

Vibristika, a pharma researcher completed her Ph.D. in the area of Phloroglucinol compounds of natural origin. She was very much interested in working further in the area as she found the work quite interesting. However, to her disappointment not many labs or institutes were working in the area, in her country. Despite her best efforts, she was unable to locate a suitable employer. Then one day, she accidentally came across an article on IPRs and found the same interesting. She started exploring the patent databases, visiting the sites as given in the article. To her joy, she was able to specifically locate pharma companies as well as research institutes, working in the area close to her heart! She was missing out the same, as she had confined herself only to literature search, while a whole 'unexplored' world lay in the patent databases. From the patents on pholoroglucinols, she was able to locate the addresses of specific companies. She wrote to them and within a few weeks, got a very positive response from several companies worldwide.

Analysis: *Knowledge of IPRs was helpful to a researcher infinding other groups working in her area of interest.*

Significance for Business Managers/Technopreneurs

1. **Enhancing business profits:** IPRs are powerful tools for enhancing business profits (details given below, under separate heading)

2. **Strategic Business Planning:** IPRs reveal upcoming and emerging technologies, much before they are actually commercialized.

They can thus be powerful tools in strategic business planning, enabling a company to focus on technologies of the future.

3. **Protection of existing markets**: Technologies influence markets. Knowledge of patents can help a business manager to protect existing markets for his products, by being alert to new developments in existing product line.

4. **Preventing infringements**: Knowledge and awareness of IPRs helps business managers to prevent infringements, thus avoiding expensive and time consuming litigation.

5. **Focus on R&D in select areas**: Knowledge of IPRs can help a company focus on select areas of R&D- those which are 'hot', which can lead to strong patents or those in which technologies can be licensed.

6. **Global partner identification**: Patents can be a very useful source of information in identifying people working in the same area or having similar commercial interests. This can help in global partnerships.

7. **100% benefits of R&D at Zero cost**: Patents are valid only in the country where they are filed, but the information is freely accessible all over the world! Thus, they enable utilization of R&D at virtually zero cost!

Role of IPRs in promoting business profits

1. **Innovations**: Owing to immense financial benefits associated with them, IPRs provide powerful incentives for invention and creation

2. **Investments**: Promote risky, costly and uncertain investments in new products and technologies by enabling the company to

fully appropriate the returns either by adoption of the technologies or by selling them.

3. **Improvements**: Stimulate improvements by 'inventing around'- encouraging others to innovate and develop alternate mechanisms to avoid infringement

4. **Markets**: Create new markets , not only for products but also for technologies

5. **Global competitiveness**: Promote Global Competitiveness- a win-win situation is created for all; Domestic firms stand to gain i) from adoption of new technologies, business methods and ideas ii) Opening up access to global markets iii) Benefit from foreign investments and collaborations, especially in high-value research or knowledge-intensive industries

6. **Information dissemination**: IPRs offer a market based mechanism for disseminating information of 'high industrial impact'.

7. **Technology Transfer**: IPRs enable technology transfer. Without rights, there can be no ownership and hence no transfer.

8. **Brand value:** IPRs help create trusted, profitable brands for domestic/global markets. Trademark protection helps to build and strengthen customer loyalty and demand, for high quality goods and services that consumers will trust and buy at home or anywhere across the globe.

Factors affecting choice of IP protection

What type of protection of IP a manager or a research professional should go in for, is a question which involves a thorough understanding of the fundamentals of IP. IP protection does not come free- money is involved. Too much of IP may not give commercial advantage, rather it may turn out to be too expensive to maintain. Therefore, ONLY that IP should be protected which is commercially relevant or consolidates hold over a particular science area. For deciding which form of IP is suitable, researchers must keep certain issues in mind:

- **Associated costs of Protection**: A patent may be easy to file but difficult to maintain. In case of international litigation, it may be next to impossible for an individual to bear the costs. Trade secret may turn out to be a better option. Another option may be to just file a patent, bring it into the public domain after publication and allow it to lapse. At least nobody else will be able to file a patent and block your entry into another country.

- **Security considerations**: Some products are impossible to protect once they are in the market, because they are easy to copy e.g. mechanical devices etc. In such cases, trade secrets have no meaning. However, in case of hi-tech products e.g. immunodiagnostic kits, copying may be very difficult and trade secrets may suffice.

- **Pace of Technological Development**: If a technology is changing very fast, than a trade secret approach would be preferable, since the information would not be leaked out at all and chances of improvement and development of new products based on disclosure of original information could be avoided.

- **Market size**: Size of market in a particular country e.g. no point in filing a patent in a country for a drug where the disease is of low prevalence.

- **Existing rivals** : Competitors to the new technology. Obviously large numbers of rivals will not make the technology commercially attractive.

- **Industrialization level**: Extent of industrialization of the country where the application is to be filed

- **Nature of product**: Are there any social issues or is it a easily acceptable product/technology having long shelf-life? What is the nature of complexity? In case of reagents, copying is not so easy but for devices, copying is comparatively easy.

Over the past few years, several international treaties administered by the World Intellectual Property Organization offer a convenient route to seek a very wide international protection of Intellectual Property. Such systems MUST be explored by researchers and used wherever possible. Some examples are:

i) **Madrid system** for the international protection of Trademarks
ii) **Hague system** for protection of industrial designs
iii) **Lisbon Agreement** for registration of appellations of origin (geographical indications)
iv) **Patent Co-operation Treaty** (PCT) for filing of patent applications with a view to obtain protection in a large number of countries

In addition, some regional offices can also be considered as they offer filing of a single application particular to a geographical or language region. Some regional offices which can be contacted are:

- **European Patent Office** (Munich, Germany)- www.european-patent-office.org
- **Eurasian Patent Office** (Moscow, Russia)- www.eapo.org
- **African Regional Industrial Property Organization** (ARIPO, Harare, Zimbabwe) -www.aripo.org
- **African Intellectual Property Organization** (OAPI, Yaounde, Cameroon)- www.oapi.wipo.net

Concluding remarks

From the illustrative stories on IPRs, importance of IPRs for business managers and its role in promoting business profitability, researchers should now be able to understand how IPRs and research work are interlinked. In addition they should be able to understand and decide suitable IP mechanisms for protecting their intellectual efforts.

****

Practice Questions

1. What are the precautions you will take, as a pharma student before you start your research work?
2. Can you file a world patent for your work? Why not?
3. How will you as a researcher, utilize your knowledge of IPRs to improve the quality of your research?
4. Can knowledge of patents be useful in career placements? How?
5. You have completed your research work and want to file a patent. What factors you will take into account while deciding to go in for a patent?
6. Express your view on 'world patent'. Are you in favour or against it ?

CHAPTER-3

How can I file a patent?

Filing a patent is a grey area for most researchers and students. In this chapter it is explained in a simple and easy manner, how a researcher can actually file a patent. Practical aspects of patenting e.g. forms, fee, precautions etc. are discussed . In addition, tips on international patenting e.g. filing a patent in Europe or USA are also discussed. Recent amendments in the Indian Patent Act and its significance for Pharma Professionals are duly covered.Basic concepts of mailbox applications or WTO applications are introduced.

3. How can I file a patent?

By understanding the steps envolved. Filing a patent is not difficult since it is a well-defined standard process. Even children can file patents! Dustin Satlof, a class 5 student of a school in Manhattan, USA received his first patent at the age of 10, for devising a new way to play a game called 'Fantasy Baseball' with special trading cards. The number of children filing patents in USA is significant enough for a new company " By Kids, For Kids" based in Stanford, USA to exclusively commercialize patented inventions of kids. Obviously, parents and trained patent attorneys must be helping the kids.

The present chapter explains the practical steps for filing a patent in India. Though the form numbers etc. may vary from country to country, the basic elements of a patent application viz. description, novelty aspects, claims etc. remain more or less the same throughout the world.

1. **What is a patent?**

   It is an exclusive right granted by the government to an inventor, for protecting his/her work from being illegally copied. The duration of a patent is quite long- twenty years!

2. **What is patentable?**

   For patentability, an invention MUST satisfy three basic criteria:

- ♣ Novelty (must be new and not known/described earlier)
- ♣ Inventive Step (must not be obvious. Must involve some effort on part of inventor)
- ♣ Industrial Application: Invention must be capable of Industrial application (must actually work and not be only theoretical).

All three criteria must be fulfilled together to enable patentability. If any one is missing, invention will not be patentable e.g. if you simply mix two formulations to get a new formulation the same will not be patentable. This is because though novelty criteria is satisfied, inventive step is missing. Similarly if you find a plant which can cure cancer, you cannot patent it.

3. What cannot be patented?

As per Indian Patent Act, 1970:

a) Something which is frivolous, contrary to public order and morality or harmful to society/environment.

b) Mere discoveries

c) Substances produced by merely mixing of components, resulting in aggregation of the properties of the components and a process for producing such substances

d) Rearrangement or duplication of known devices

e) Method of Agriculture and Horticulture, Medical treatments, plants and animals in whole, except microbes

f) Mathematical or business methods

g) Literary, aesthetic, artistic works, methods of playing games

h) Presentation of information, Topography of Circuits

i) Invention which is in fact traditional knowledge

j) Inventions pertaining to atomic energy

4. How can I patent my Invention?

- Firstly, check whether your invention does not fall in list of non-patentable inventions as given above.
- If it does not, then check whether your invention meets the three criteria of patentability viz. novelty, non-obviousness and industrial application(N.I.I).

Checking up whether your invention is really new or not (novel), can be done by performing a "Prior Art Search". In simple words, it means confirming whether what you are claiming is new, has not already been done by someone, somewhere in the world. For this you can adopt different approaches as follows:

Literature search: Perform a thorough literature search. As a researcher, you are already familiar with literature search, checking relevant journals, current contents, citation indexes etc. DO NOT UNDERESTIMATE THE IMPORTANCE OF LITERATURE SEARCH. Just because something is not in a patent database search, does not mean it is not in public domain. Someone may have just gone ahead and published it, without filing a patent!

Search of worldwide patent databases: Patent databases can be searched using appropriate keywords. It gives a very good idea of whether what you are trying to protect has already been patented or not, thus saving you time and money. Also, searching patent databases helps in familiarizing you with patent language, method of description etc. making drafting of a patent application easy.

Patent databases are free as well as paid. Some of the free patent databases are:

1. USA	www.uspto.gov
2. Europe	http://ep.espacenet.com
3. Australia	www.ipaustralia.gov.au
4. Canada	http://www.patents1.ic.gc.ca
5. Korea	http://www.kipris.or.kr
6. India	www.pfc.org.in/db

Two other good online patent databases are :

1. STN	www.stn-international.de
2. Delphion	www.delphion.com

but both are paid. Limited searches can be carried out free during the trial period.

5. What next?

You have checked literature, searched patent databases and found that your invention is truly novel. What next? Find out under which patent office your state lies. There are four patent offices in India- Kolkata (Head Office), Mumbai, Chennai and Delhi. Each has a particular jurisdiction as follows:

1. **Mumbai**: Maharashtra, Gujrat, MP, Goa and the Union Territories of Daman and Diu, Dadra and Nagar Haveli
2. **Chennai**: AP, Kerala, Tamil Nadu, Mysore, Union Territories of Pondicherry, Laccadive, Minicoy and Aminidevi Islands
3. **Delhi**: Punjab, Haryana, Himachal Pradesh, J&K, Rajasthan, UP, Union Territories of Chandigarh and Delhi
4. **Kolkata**: Rest of India

Once you have determined which patent office to submit your patent application to, the next step is to draft a patent application.

6. What does a patent application consist of ?

If you are filing a patent application in India, your application will consist of four forms viz. Form 1, Form 2, Form 3, Form 5 and Form 18 (Duly filled formats are given in Annexure -1). These forms are not available commercially, but the formats are standard and can be retyped. While forms 1, 3, 5 and 18 are simple consisting of just 1 or 2 pages, Form 2 is the one which constitutes the 'heart' of the patent and contains a detailed description of the invention, drawings, examples and claims.

In Form 2, a set pattern of headings for describing the invention is followed viz.

- Field of the invention,
- Background of the Invention,
- Objects of the Invention,
- Summary of the Invention
- Detailed description
- Examples
- Claims
- Figures/Drawings if any
- Abstract

All forms must be filed in DUPLICATE, when submitting to the patent office.

7. Do I have to hire a Lawyer to file a patent applica tion?

No, you can file a patent application directly. Though it is not compulsory to hire a lawyer, it is usually a good idea to hire one. The attorney is familiar with the legal language and can help in better drafting of claims without leaving any loopholes which can be challenged later. Secondly, he can deal with various objections raised by the examiner during the course of examination of your patent and send proper replies. Lastly, being a professional, he increases the chances for the successful grant of a patent.

8. How do I find a suitable patent attorney ?

An ordinary lawyer cannot help you with the filing of a patent application. You will need the services of a patent attorney. Usually a list of patent attorneys of a country is available from the patent office free of charge. In India the list is availble at www.patentoffice.nic.in. The patent office will however not guide you regarding which attorney to hire nor will it provide details about attorney fees. You must contact different attorneys and find out which one suits you. Make a wise decision when selecting an attorney- don't hesitate to ask how many applications he has filed, success rate etc. Ask him about few of his previous clients and check up whether they are satisfied with his services. Also, ALWAYS ask about charges and get list of charges in writing. Be clear whether charges indicated include the Govt./official fee or not. Clarity of money involved can help you in proper planning of your budget and ensure you are able to make prompt and timely payments to your attorney for services rendered.

9. What is the cost of filing a patent application and other related expenses?

The cost will depend upon whether you are filing the application as an individual or as an organization. To encourage individual inventors, the fee for individuals is much lower. Presently, the official fee for filing an Indian patent application is Rs.1000/- (for individuals) and Rs.4000/- (for corporates/organizations). Under the amended patent rules, 2006 request for examination on Form 18 has to be filed for the application to be examined. Fee for examination is Rs.2500/- for individuals and Rs.10,000/- for corporates. Thus, as an individual your initial filing expenses on account of fee alone will be Rs.3500/-, while that for corporates it will be Rs.14,000/-.

Attorney Fee for drafting and filing generally ranges from Rs.10000/- to Rs.15,000/-. However, there are other charges also involved subsequently e.g for replying to examiners objections and filing reply, seeking extension of time etc.and these range from Rs.1500/- to Rs.2000/- per action. Finally, a patent is granted for which NO FEE IS INVOLVED. Earlier sealing fee had to be paid, but this has now been waived off.

This is not all. Even after you are granted a patent, you have to pay a maintenance fee at regular intervals or your patent will lapse. For first five years fee is Rs.500/- per year and Rs.2000/- per year for individuals and corporates respectively. For next five years it is Rs.1500/- and Rs.6000/- per year (till 10th year), for next five years Rs.3000/- and Rs.12,000/- and for last five years Rs.5000/- and 20,000/- respectively. Thus, the cost of filing a patent application may not be much, but getting a patent and maintaining it may turn out to be quite expensive. Usually, it is a good idea as an individual to protect your invention by filing a patent and immediately make efforts to find a buyer. In that case, remaining expenses can be borne by the buyer.

10. Do I have to deposit the patent application per sonally at the patent office or can I send it by post ?

No, you don't have to deposit the patent application in person. You can send it by registered/speed-post. The prescribed fee can be sent in the form of a Bank Draft, payable to the Controller of Patents of the respective office where you are sending the application.

11. What happens after I have deposited the patent application?

You are issued a receipt by the patent office, bearing a patent application number and date of filing. This receipt is important and must be preserved carefully by you. It is legal proof of your rights over the invention for which you have filed the patent. The patent application number is important- you must quote it in all future correspondence with the patent office regarding your patent.

12. I have an idea which I want to protect- can I do it?

Yes, by filing a provisional patent application. Format is the same as for the complete patent application, only detailed description and claims are omitted. However, your idea and the preliminary work carried out is described. Fee for filing a provisional application and complete application is the same ie. Rs.1000/- (individuals) and Rs.4000/- (corporates). However, when complete application is filed after filing provisional, no official fee is charged by the govt. Attorneys usually charge some fee (varying from Rs.1500/- to Rs.5000/-) for filing a complete application after provisional. Usually the benefit of filing a provisional application is during M.Sc./Ph.D work where some interesting findings may be there, but sufficient data is not available. Filing a provisional application protects your work, while giving you time to generate data. Final application/complete specifications must be filed within one year.

13. How long does it take to get a patent ?

By Normal route: Approximately 30 months

Explanation: Application is filed and published after 18 months in

Journal of Patent Office. It CANNOT BE EXAMINED before publication, so 18 months gone! Thereafter examination is requested by you, by paying fee of Rs. 2500/- (individual)/Rs.10,000/- (corporate). Examination starts and has to be completed within 12 months. Hence 18+12 = 30 months (2.5 years) is the normal minimum period for grant of patent. If examination is completed early e.g. within six months, then patent grant occurs within 18+6 = 24 months (2 years).

By Fast route: Approximately 12-15 months

Explanation: Since patent examination will not start before publication, one can expedite patent grant process by requesting EARLY PUBLICATION (Fee Rs. 2500/- (individual)/Rs.10,000/- (corporate). Normally, this fee DOES NOT have to be paid, since application will be published after 18 months anyway. Once early publication occurs (3-4 months), examination fee is paid and examination starts. It may be completed in 6-12 months. Thus, by fast route, patent can be granted to you within 12-15 months.

Time taken during patent examination - why?

- After you have submitted your application in the patent office and it is published, examination starts.
- Depending upon the area in which your invention falls, it goes to the appropriate expert.
- He then gives his comments and sends your application back with comments. If your application is well-drafted and easy to understand, examiner will have less objections and acceptance will be fast.
- If your application is hard to understand, then it will take time to clear the objections and your application will get delayed.
- To explain, you may have to conduct interview with the examiner. This is the reason, why it takes time for a patent to be granted.

- REMEMBER, once a patent is granted, you have rights for TWENTY YEARS over it, which is a long period. Hence, patent is examined very carefully and it takes time to grant it!

14. For how long is a patent valid ?

Twenty years, provided you pay the maintenance fee regularly every year. Otherwise it will lapse.

15. Can I file a 'world patent'?

There is no such thing as a 'world patent'. However, if you do file a patent abroad, it will be called an 'international patent'. If you want to protect you invention in a number of countries you can file a patent under the 'Patent Co-operation Treaty'(PCT). Under PCT you can file a single application for patents in a number of countries. The grant of patent will be done individually by each country, but you will save time and money since a single filing will be valid in several countries. At present there are nearly 140 countries which are covered under PCT.

16. What is a "Convention Patent Application"?

There are 176 countries which have been designated by the Indian Govt. as convention countries. Under the agreement, if an Indian after filing an application in India, files an application within 12 months in any of these countries, he gets the benefit of priority filing from the date he filed in India. An application filed under this agreement is called a convention patent application.

17. What is the difference between a "design patent" and a "utility patent?"

These terms are not in use in India, but in the USA. A design patent protects only the external features of a product. Its equivalent intellectual property protection mechanism in India is "industrial design registration". What is of critical importance is 'utility patent' in which the invention is protected as a whole, not just the external features.

18. What is a "patent of addition"?

After filing a patent, if an inventor makes an improvement which was not disclosed in the original patent application, he can file a 'patent of addition'. This must be filed only after filing 'complete specification'. The term of the patent of addition runs for the same period as that of the main patent. Patent of addition is granted ONLY after grant of the main patent and not beforehand. Supposing a patent is already granted and then improvement is made by same inventor. He can file patent of addition and claim benefit from priority date of the parent patent. However, the protection he will get is for the remaining period only. Supposing you apply for a patent in 2003 and are granted a patent in 2006, 3 years have already gone. If after two years of further R&D, you want to apply for a patent of addition, term will be for remaining period of the parent patent.

19. What is a "divisional patent"?

When a patent application contains more than one invention, the applicant may file a separate application for the second invention. This application 'divided' out of the parent application, will be called a 'divisional patent'. It contains ALL information disclosed in the parent application, but is filed as a separate application for greater clarity. Reference to the main patent is made in the body of the divisional patent applicaton.

20. From where can I obtain information about patents?

Some useful websites are:

1. www.patentoffice.nic.in
2. http://ipindia.nic.in
3. www.wipo.org
4. www.bpmlegal.com

International Patenting

A critical aspect of patents which every researcher must understand is that 'patents are valid only in the country where they are filed and nowhere else.' Hence, a patent filed in USA is valid only in USA but not in Europe. It can be freely copied in Europe without the need for any permission. If a researcher feels that his invention is good, has lots of commercial value then he has to go in for international patenting in several countries. Pharma patents at times may have significant value, making it very important for a researcher to understand the fundamentals of International Patenting.

1. Why should I go in for an international patent?

Because a national patent is valid only in the country where it is filed. If your invention is good, has significant commercial value worldwide, then restricting your rights to only one country (national) does not make good commercial sense. You must file an international patent or make use of the Patent Co-operation Treaty (PCT) to secure patent rights in multiple countries.

2. In how many countries should I file an international patent?

It depends upon several factors e.g. your budget, value of your invention, likely market of your invention and location of potential buyers. However, the single most important factor which decides whether you should file an international patent or not, depends upon where the likely buyers for the patent are located. If buyers for your patent are mainly in USA, you may wish to file patent only in the USA. However, if your invention has application in a particular country e.g. a drug for malaria, which is for a disease prevalent mainly in the Asian Region, you may wish to file in Asian countries rather than USA and Europe, where you may not find buyers for your patent. So, ultimately, it is the potential market for your patent which decides in which countries you should file.

3. What is PCT?

PCT stands for Patent Co-operation Treaty. Initiated in the year 1970, it is an agreement signed by more than a hundred countries, to facilitate the filing of international patents by inventors. It is administered by the World Intellectual Property Organization (WIPO), a specialized agency of the United Nations having headquarters at Geneva, Switzerland. PCT implements the concept of a single international application, valid in member countries of PCT. The number of countries signatory to PCT now stands at nearly 140. Apart from simplification of the patent filing procedure, another aim of PCT is to promote easy exchange of technical information between different countries, by providing a common platform for publication of patent applications from different countries. Details about PCT are available at http://www.wipo.int/pct/en/

4. What are the advantages of PCT filing of a patent application ?

PCT filing offers several practical advantages:

1. You can designate nearly 140 countries under PCT. Practically, this means your rights exist in all the countries for the period allowed under PCT i.e. 30 months or 2.5 years.
2. Entry into national phases gets delayed by 2.5 years, which you can utilize to search for buyers of your patent. If you are working in an industry, filing a patent through PCT helps in your rights getting protected in the respective countries.
3. Entry into national phases of multiple countries becomes easier, since search report is already with you and you know the chances of getting a patent successfully, in minimum time and at minimum expense, once you enter the national phase.

5. Will patent granted by PCT be called a PCT patent?

There is no such thing as a PCT patent. PCT is not a 'patent granting' process. It is merely a common filing procedure agreed upon by more than a hundred countries, to avoid duplication of work and also to help inventors. PCT does not grant any patents. Under the PCT system, instead of filing multiple applications, an applicant can file a single application, which protects his rights TEMPORARILY in all the designated countries, till the time he enters the national phase of the countries.

6. What is the procedure an applicant will go through, if he files a PCT application?

A researcher or an applicant can file a PCT application only if his country is a member of the PCT. Firstly, he would have to file an application with the receiving office, usually the patent office in his home country. Then his application would pass through two distinct phases- international phase and national phase. The international phase includes four steps: Filing, International Search (to determine novelty), international publication and international preliminary examination. While the first three steps automatically take place once applicant has paid the fee, the fourth step ie. international preliminary examination is optional and will occur only if the applicant specifically asks for it and pays the required fee. It is relevant to mention here that the search report is sufficiently detailed and gives an applicant a fairly good idea about the patentability of his invention and his chances of being awarded a patent successfully.

Thus, we can say that during the international phase, a PCT application will go through 3 distinct steps-

- filing,
- search and
- publication.

If after the international phase, an applicant wishes to proceed ONLY THEN will the NATIONAL PHASE of the PCT application be there. The decision regarding in which countries an inventor wants to file his patent after PCT, must be taken within 30 months of priority date i.e. the date when the application was first filed by inventor (for some countries, this period is 21 months). If this 30 month period expires, inventor cannot enter into national phase of any of the designated countries and all his efforts and expenses at patenting will go waste.

7. When can I avoid filing through PCT?

When you feel that you want to file in just one or two countries and not multiple countries. In fact, once a patent is filed by you, in your respective country, next step is to move internationally, if you think it has commercial value. For moving internationally, you can use two approaches:

1. File individually in the countries you are interested
2. File through PCT

If you want to target just the USA and Europe (which most inventors do!), then DO NOT proceed through the PCT. Just proceed directly and save the money you would spend on PCT filing. However, if you feel your invention and business interests have worldwide importance, then choose PCT.

8. What are the factors to be taken into consideration, when going in for National Phase Filings after PCT?

1. Whether the countries where you wish to seek patent protection,have any commercial importance for your invention?
2. How much will be the budget? Can you afford it?
3. Which regional offices you want to use, for entry into national phases?
4. Which attorneys you want to choose, to represent you?

After PCT, the most convenient and easy route for entry into the national phase can be by using the REGIONAL OFFICES ROUTE. The following regional offices exist:

- European Patent Office (Munich, Germany)- www.european-patent-office.org
- Eurasian Patent Office (Moscow, Russia)- www.eapo.org
- African Regional Industrial Property Organization (ARIPO, Harare, Zimbabwe) -www.aripo.org
- African Intellectual Property Organization (OAPI, Yaounde, Cameroon)- www.oapi.wipo.net

9. Is there any possibility of a World Patent?

Firstly, as on today there is no such thing as a 'WORLD PATENT'. It simply does not exist. Each country grants patents individually and protection coverage too is restricted to national level. However, the concept does have advantages:

- Rapid- drastic reduction in time, as duplication of efforts involved in granting patents would be avoided (Example- Personal case. US patent was granted after 4 years of filing. Indian Patent Office after 6 years took up the case and proceeded fresh. Refused to recognize the patent granted by US and examiner raised fresh objections. Inventor has already spent money getting US patent. Now again he had to spend time and money to get patent in India for the same invention!)
- Cost-effective- Dramatically reduced costs on account of filing and maintenance
- Helps avoid duplication of efforts

This would greatly benefit small inventors and business entities which find it difficult to bear the prohibitive costs of international patenting, in different countries. Also, setting up of a world patent system has huge implications. It would replace the current situation where each country has its own laws, own patent office and own courts. It would end the flexibility available under TRIPS as the rules would be applicable globally. Hence, there are genuine concerns that interests of developing countries might be compromised.

World Patent- Initiatives undertaken

The Director General of World Intellectual Property Organization (WIPO) has announced a new initiative- the WIPO Patent Agenda, for preparing the blueprint of a international, unified patent system. Under this system inventors and industry would have access to national, regional and internationally effective patent systems to enable them to obtain, maintain and enforce their patents globally. Though at present no such system exists, some sort of common protection is available through:

- Patent Cooperation Treaty (PCT)
- Patent Law Treaty (PLT)
- Agreement on Trade Related Aspects of Intellectual Property Rights (TRIPS)

PCT : As discussed, PCT is simply a common 'filing procedure' for international patents monitored and executed by WIPO.

- Under PCT an applicant does not have to file separate applications in each country in which he wants protection- the same set of applications as filed under PCT is submitted.
- Secondly, repeated prior art search is avoided. A single recognized international authority conducts prior art search and the results are acceptable to all countries in which application is submitted for grant of patent.
- However, patent is granted individually by each country. Fee etc. too has to be paid individually for each country.

PCT offers advantage to the applicants by giving them sufficient time to assess the market potential of their patent in different countries and to rethink their commercial strategies before proceeding for national filing. A PCT application is published as a WO (For WIPO) document.

Advantages of PCT

- Simplification of paperwork
- Reduced costs
- Reduction in time for obtaining protection for inventions throughout the world
- Dynamic- reforms are constantly being undertaken e.g. Treaty was amended in 1979, 1984 and again in 2001.

Having being in operation for several years, PCT is becoming increasingly popular amongst member countries.

Patent Law Treaty (PLT)

Basically, it is "an offshoot of PCT which aims at further simplification of patent protection procedures by streamlining and harmonizing formal requirements related to patents or patent procedures". PLT defines a set of rules on how to prepare, file and manage patents in all the member countries that sign on. PLT was adopted in Geneva on 1st June, 2000 but is NOT YET IN FORCE.

Benefits

- **Easier access to global IPP**: Harmonization of procedures under national laws is expected to result in easier access to worldwide patent protection and cost reduction for applicants.
- **Cost Reduction**: Reduction of administrative costs of patent offices of both industrialized and developing countries, the benefit of which could be passed on to applicants in the form of lower fee.

Substantive Patent Law Treaty (SPLT)

Harmonization of various patent laws of different countries is aimed to be achieved through the Substantive Patent Law Treaty (SPLT). SPLT is an affixed set of rules on what can be patented and under what conditions. It is not a binding treaty yet and all negotiations pertaining to it are being carried out under the WIPO standing committee on the law of patents (SCP). The SCP aims at creation of substantive patent law standards pertaining to issues of :

- Prior art
- Novelty
- Utility and inventiveness
- Requirements relating to sufficient disclosure
- Drafting of claims
- Interpretation of claims
- Grounds for refusal of an application
- Grounds for refusal, revocation and invalidation of a patent

Thus , gradually an opinion is being built up for a SINGLE PATENT LAW relying on mutually agreed procedures, which could be administered by the WIPO. However, one must remain alert to the fact that interests of the developing countries are not jeopardized.

Agreement on Trade Related Aspects of Intellectual Property Rights (TRIPS)

This agreement is also a step forward in achieving the goal of a 'world patent'. Under this agreement, minimum international standards for :

- Patentable subject matter
- Disclosure requirements
- Patent Rights
- Limitations on those rights
- Means for enforcing those rights

have already been introduced.

However, this agreement is not absolute.

- It gives members a certain amount of authority and flexibility regarding execution of these rights e.g. though the TRIPS agreement states that patents shall be available in all fields of technology, at the same time it empowers members to stop patents from being granted if commercialization of those patents would offend morality or public order.
- It also allows member countries to exclude plants and animals from patentability as a matter of principle.

The minimum set of standards created by TRIPS agreement are building harmony into patent laws of the WTO members.

Regional Patent Offices- roads to a 'world patent office'

It is important to note that steps towards harmonization and execution of patent laws have already been taken with the establishment of Regional Patent Offices, under which patent applications which are filed offer protection throughout a particular REGION and not just a COUNTRY. This helps reduce costs and workload associated with national patent systems.

Some of the regional patent offices which have already been established are as follows:

- ARIPO- African Regional Intellectual Property Organization
- EPO- European Patent Office
- EAPO- Eurasian Patent Office
- OAPI- African Intellectual Property Organization

Recent Amendments (2005) in the Indian Patents Act and its significance for Pharma Researchers

The most significant aspect of recent amendments in the Indian Patent Act have been the provision of allowing PRODUCT PATENTS to pharma products, which was not allowed earlier. It is important to remember that product patents always existed in India- only they were not allowed for pharmaceutical products, owing to concerns by the government that the same would lead to increase in drug prices.

Three issues in the Indian context, were prominent following the TRIPS agreement in 1995:

1. **Extension of term of all patents to 20 years.**
   Previously, patent term in India was 14 years. However, for pharma processes, patent term was only 7 years and for pharma products, NO PATENTS WERE ALLOWED. Now for Pharma process patents also, the term has been increased to 20 years from the earlier 7 years.
2. **Granting of product patents to pharma products.**
   Under the Indian Patent Act, prior to TRIPS, product patents were not allowed for Pharma products. However, under the modified act, product patents have been allowed for pharma products.
3. **Introduction of temporary provision of EMRs (Exclusive Marketing Rights) during the transition period (1995-2005):**
   Patents filed during this period were called 'mailbox applications' or 'black-box' applications or 'WTO applications'. Since these patents could be examined only after Jan, 2005 but some protection had to be given to inventors, the concept of EMRs was introduced under which an inventor could apply to the controller of patents and seek 'exclusive' rights for marketing his invention in India, for a MAXIMUM OF FIVE YEARS ONLY. EMRs was a self-extinguishing mechanism, which came to an end on 1st January 2005 when product patents came into force in India.

AN OVERVIEW OF THE AMENDMENTS

The salient features of the Patents (Amendment) Act, 2005 with special reference to the Pharma Industry are as follows:

- **Product patents**: have been introduced in all fields of technology. Accordingly, inventions in areas such as chemicals, food and pharmaceuticals hitherto entitled to process patents would now become eligible for product patent protection also. However, salts, esters, ethers, polymorphs, metabolites, pure form, particle size, isomers, mixtures of isomers, complexes, combinations and other derivatives of a known substance have been excluded from patentability unless they differ significantly in properties with regard to efficacy.
- **New Use of existing pharma product**: According to earlier law, any new use of a known substance was not patentable. The Ordinance clarifies that only "mere new use" of a known substance is not patentable to prevent patenting of obvious or known applications of a known substance.
- **Patentability of software**: The original provision prohibiting the patentability of inventions relating to computer programmes per se has been reinstated. Thus, computer programmes per se do not come within the purview of patent protection. However, software which is an inherent part of a machine or a device is patentable.
- **EMRs eliminated**: The facility relating to Exclusive Marketing Rights ('EMRs') and a transitional provision for an automatic and priority examination process for black box applications linked to EMR applications has been discontinued.
- **Opposition**: Both pre-grant and post-grant opposition allowed. Within 3 months after publication a person can file application for opposition. At any time after grant of patent, but before expiry

of one year from date of publication of grant of patent, person can oppose a patent.

- **Compulsory licensing**: A provision for enabling grant of compulsory licenses for export of medicines to countries which have insufficient or lack of manufacturing capacity for meeting public health emergencies has been introduced (in line with the Doha Declaration).
- **Infringements**: The law also enables a claim for damages in an infringement action retrospectively from the date of publication and not from the date of acceptance of the patent application as was provided earlier. However, in the case of Black Box applications, damages can be claimed only from the date of grant of patent.
- **Mail-box applications**: A patent holder in respect of a patent granted on a Black Box application, is prohibited from instituting an infringement suit against enterprises which have made significant investment and were producing and marketing the concerned product prior to January 1, 2005 and which continue to manufacture the product covered by the patent on the date of grant of the patent. The patent holder shall only be entitled to receive reasonable royalty from such enterprises.
- **Inventive step**: The definition of 'inventive step' has been modified to - 'a feature of an invention that involves technical advance as compared to the existing knowledge or having economic significance or both and that makes the invention not obvious to a person skilled in the art'.
- **Pharmaceutical Substances**: The new definition of 'pharmaceutical substances' is - 'any new entity involving one or more inventive steps'.
- **Fast -track granting introduced**: A provision for requesting early publication of an application has been introduced.

- **Time period of request for examination reduced**: Request for examination of an application to be made after publication of the application but within thirty six months from the priority date or date of filing of application, whichever is earlier, as opposed to the earlier period of forty eight months from the filing date.
- **Time period for examination and grant reduced**: The time frame for putting an application in order for acceptance subsequent to its first examination has been further shortened to 6 months, extendible by three months, from the date on which the first statement of objection is issued. The time frame for putting an application in order for grant (which has been examined before January 1, 2005) remains a non-extendible twelve months.
- **Indian filing compulsory**: Provisions relating to 'first filing' in India for an Indian resident with respect to an application relating to any invention have been re-introduced.
- **Revision in Fees**: Substantive increase in official fee in respect of various activities, for example, an additional official fee will now be levied in all cases where the pages of specification exceed 30 (Rs. 400 per page for corporates) and the number of claims exceed 10 (Rs.800 per claim). This system did not exist earlier.

However, considerable relief has also been granted under the new patent amendments.

- The requirement of payment of a patent sealing fee (Rs.5000/ for corporates) has been dispensed with.
- The fee for compulsory licensing has been drastically reduced fromRs.75,000 earlier to only Rs.6000/-/

MAILBOX APPLICATIONS - BASIC CONCEPTS

Mailbox applications were a special set of patent applications, filed in India after the year 1995 and referred specifically to applications for product patents in the area of pharmaceutical and agrochemical products.

India signed the Trade Related Intellectual Property Rights (TRIPS) agreement, in 1995. Under the TRIPS agreement, it was mandatory to change Indian Patent Rules to bring them in conformity with international Rules. Since IP protection was governed by national laws, these could only be changed by appropriate legislation, which obviously was a time consuming task. Accordingly, a ten year transition period was allowed to all countries member to the agreement, to make their laws compliant with the TRIPS agreement. This period came to an end on 31st December, 2004 and product patents for drugs and agrochemicals came into force in India from 1st January, 2005. This was a very significant change for the Indian pharma industry, which stood 'accused' of copying drugs, since in area of drugs, only process and not product patents were allowed. Even in case of process patents, the duration had been 'shortened' under Indian patent rules- only 7 years from date of filing or 5 years from date of grant, whichever was shorter. However, under the TRIPS agreement, both these 'benefits' have gone- term of all patents (irrespective of process or product) has been uniformly increased to 20 years and product patents have also been allowed for drugs.

What are the implications of the new patent amendments, for Indian Pharma Industry, especially in the context of drug patenting? How many patent applications were there in the mailbox? Can the manufacturers be penalized for manufacturing drugs, which are covered by patent applications which have now come out of the 'mailbox'? What are the fears and risks which need to be addressed? These are some of the issues which are discussed below for the benefit of pharma students and researchers.

Mailbox Protection- What is it? What was the need?

Mailbox protection was a mechanism under the TRIPS agreement under which countries not implementing product patent protection as on 1st January, 1995, provided a facility for FILING of PRODUCT patent applications for pharmaceuticals and agrochemicals. Technically speaking, since the patent rules in India had not yet been modified to allow product patents in 1995, product applications for pharmaceutical and agrochemicals could not be filed. However, since we were a signatory to TRIPS, we could not refuse applications for such patents also. Hence, 'mailbox protection' was a temporary mechanism, under which patent applications were just received and filed for TEN YEARS, till the product patents came into force. These applications were also called "Black Box " or " WTO applications" and merely indicated that these were the applications which would not be examined till product patents came into force.

How was protection offered to an Inventor, who had filed a 'mailbox patent application' in India?

It was a fact that a mailbox applicant in India legally had no rights, since his application had been merely received, but neither examined nor granted any patent. To compensate for the same, the concept of EMR (Exclusive Marketing Rights) was introduced, under which an applicant could be provided exclusive rights to market his product in India for a period of FIVE YEARS. To receive the benefit of TRIPS provision for marketing exclusivity in a developing country, certain provisions had to be fulfilled by the applicant:

(i) He should have applied for and BEEN GRANTED a patent in another member country which had signed TRIPS.

(ii) He should have been granted MARKETING APPROVAL in both the other country as well as India, after January, 1995.

It is interesting to note that EMR was a 'self-extinguishing' mechanism, only meant to provide temporary relief. It no longer exists today, since we have already introduced product patents.

What is the status of Mailbox applications in India?

A total of 8926 patent applications were filed in the mailbox. Major filings were done by foreign entities(7520) and remaining were Indian applications(1406). Out of these, total applications in Pharma segment were 7152, of which foreign were 5852 and Indian were 1300.

Table: Status of Mailbox Applications filed in India (Source: Financial Express, 21st April, 2005)

Total Mailbox Applications	**8926**
Foreign	7520
Indian	1406
Total Pharma Mailbox Applications	**7152**
Foreign Pharma applications US - 2096 Germany - 1134 UK - 573 Switzerland - 538 Japan - 434 Sweden - 351 France - 278 Denmark - 278 Belgium - 170	5852
Indian Pharma	1300

A pharma Industry is manufacturing a drug for which mailbox application was filed. Can the Industry be penalized?

No. The Indian Patent Act, 2005 provides that mailbox patent grantees cannot file a suit for infringement against an infringer who has made significant investments and was producing and marketing the concerned product prior to 1st January, 2005 and also continues to manufacture and sell the product covered by the patent on the date of grant of patent. The only consolation offered to such mailbox patentee in the face of such infringement is that the patent grantee can claim reasonable royalty from the infringer. The main idea behind this amendment is to allow the on-going production of drugs, make the drugs available at a reasonable price and to protect the employment and investments made in the manufacture of such drugs.

What will be the term of the patent granted for mailbox applications?
Unlike the normal patents in which term of patents is 20 years from date of filing, in case of mailbox applications an exception has been made. The term for the patent WILL NOT BE FROM DATE OF FILING but from date of grant of patent. Hence, no remedy would be available for infringing acts done prior to the date of grant of patent.

Example: Supposing you as an inventor filed a patent application for a drug on Jan, 2000. On opening the mailbox in January, 2005 your application got examined and subsequently you got patent in 2006. Then actual term of patent should have been twenty years from date of filing ie. till 2020. However, since for mailbox applications, term is being determined not from date of filing but from date of GRANT, ie. 2006 therefore effective term of patent will only be 2020-2006 i.e.14years.

Now that product patents have come into force, will manufacturing and prices of existing drugs be affected?
It is important to understand that product patents do not automatically translate into drugs. The road from filing a product patent to actually

bringing a drug into the market is quite long- involving R&D work, clinical trials, regulatory approvals etc. Assuming 8-10 years for completion of the above, the effective life of a product patent can range from 10-12 years only. Also, patents are NOT RETROSPECTIVE but are always prospective ie. existing products are NOT AFFECTED. Hence, product patents have no bearing on existing drugs being manufactured.

Apart from the short patent term which is remaining, by the time a drug clears trials and regulatory approvals, another important aspect also keeps a check on prices- the new drug has to compete with many other existing drugs, within the same therapeutic segment ie. generics.

Technically, all drugs being manufactured in India before January 2005 can be effectively classified as 'generic drugs' (generic drugs are those which are off-patent or not under patent control). This is because the country did not grant product patents prior to January, 2005. Secondly, mailbox applications though accepted in the patent office, were to be examined only after January, 2005. During this period, even those drugs for which patent application had been filed, could be freely manufactured, since applications had not be examined, published or granted patents.

Now under the amended patents act, 2005 it has been specified that manufacturers making drugs, for which patent applications had been filed in the mailbox, will not be penalized and may continue to manufacture the same, after paying reasonable royalty to the original patentee. Hence, this practically means that all drugs prior to 2005 can be classified in 'generics category'. Thus, fears regarding negative affect of product patents on either manufacturing or prices of existing drugs are unfounded.

Suggested readings/ site visits:

1. WIPO moves towards 'world patent system'
   http://www.grain.org/publications/wipo.patent.2002

2. WIPO Patent Agenda
http://patentagenda.wipo.int/index.html
3. Patent agenda overview
http://www.wipo.int/patent/agenda/en/index.html
4. PCT reform
http://www.wipo.int/pct/reform/en/index.html
5. Official outlines of the US goals for a global patent system
http://usinfo.state.gov/topical/econ/ipr/ipr-rogan26.htm
6. Correa Carlos et al. The WIPO patent agenda: The risks for developing countries.
http://www.southcentre.org/publications/wipopatent/wipopatent-03.htm
7. *www.ipindia.nic.in*

Practice Questions

1. What are the three essential criteria for filing a patent?
2. Is a patent filed in India, also valid in the USA?
3. You are an Indian Citizen. Can you seek patent rights in Europe?
4. How much time does it take to get a patent?
5. How much budget should you plan, if you as an inventor want to file a patent in the USA and India?
6. Your friend tells you he got a PCT patent. What will be your response?
7. Can you patent a drug in India?
8. Is it possible to protect the process for manufacturing a drug, whose patent has expired?
9. What are mailbox applications?
10. What IP mechanisms can you use to protect generic drugs?

ANNEXURE-1
FORMAT OF PATENT APPLICATION AND TEMPLATES OF FORMS FOR FILING IN INDIA

A patent application in India consists of a set of four forms viz. Forms 1, 2, 3 and 5 submitted in duplicate to the respective patent office, alongwith fee. Form 18 is required at a later stage after publication of the patent application (18 months).

Duly filled formats are given below to enable readers to understand and make use of the templates.

Using these forms as templates, readers can easily fill in details and file their own patent applications.

Illustrative duly filled format of Patent Application Form in India

FORM 1 **THE PATENTS ACT 1970** **(39 of 1970)** **&** **The Patents Rules, 2003** **APPLICATION FOR GRANT OF PATENT** *[(See section 7,54 & 135 and rule 20(1)]*	**(FOR OFFICE USE ONLY)** Application No: Filing Date: Amount of Fee Paid: CBR No: Signature

1. APPLICANT (S):

Name	Nationality	Address
National Institute of Pharmaceutical Education and Research, Mohali, India	-	NIPER, Phase X, Mohali-160062 INDIA

2. INVENTOR (S):

Name	Nationality	Address
1. **Dr.Parikshit Bansal**	INDIAN	Deptt. Of Pharmaceutical Technology, NIPER, Phase X, Mohali-160062

3. TITLE OF THE INVENTION: IMPROVED COLUMN FOR CHROMATOGRAPHY

4. ADDRESS FOR CORRESPONDENCE OF APPLICANT/ **Dr.Parikshit Bansal** Deptt. Of Pharmaceutical Technology NIPER, Phase X, Mohali-160062	Tel: Off. 0172-2214683-87 ext. 2123

5. PRIORITY PARTICULARS OF THE APPLICATION (S) FILED IN CONVENTION COUNTRY:

Country	Application No.	Filing Date	Name of Applicant	Title of the invention

6. PARTICULARS FOR FILING PATENT COOPERATION TREATY (PCT) NATIONAL PHASE APPLICATION:

International Application No.	International filing date as allotted by the receiving office

7. PARTICULARS FOR FILING DIVISIONAL APPLICATION:

Original (First) Application No.	Date of filing of Original (First) Application
Nil	Nil

8. PARTICULARS FOR FILING PATENT OF ADDITION:

Main Application / Patent No.	Date of filing of Main Application
Nil	Nil

9. DECLARATIONS:

(i) Declaration by the Inventor(s)

I/We, the above named inventor(s) is/are the true & first inventor(s) for this invention and declare that the applicant(s) herein is/are my/our assignee or legal representative.

(a) Date:

(b) Signature(s) ___________

(ii) Declaration by the Applicant(s) in the convention country

I/We, the Applicant(s) in the convention country declare that the applicant(s) herein is/are my/our assignee or legal representative.

(a) Date:
(b) Signature(s)
(c) Name(s)

(iii) Declaration by the Applicant(s)

I/We, the Applicant(s) hereby declare(s) that:-

- I am / We are in possession of the above-mentioned invention
- The provisional / complete specification relating to the invention is filed with this application
- The invention as disclosed in the specification uses the biological material from India and the necessary permission from the competent authority shall be submitted by me/us before the grant of patent to me/us.
- There is no lawful ground of objection to the grant of the Patent to me/us.
- I am/We are the assignee or legal representative of true & first inventors
- the application or each of the applications, particulars of which are given in Para-5 was the first application in convention country/countries in respect of my/our invention.
- I/We claim the priority from the above mentioned application(s0 filed in convention country/countries and state that no application for protection in respect of the invention had been made in a convention country before that date by me/us or by any person from which I/We derive the title
- My/our application in India is based on international application under Patent Cooperation Treaty (PCT) as mentioned in Para-6
- The application is divided out of my/our application particulars of which are given in Para-7 and pray that this application may be treated as deemed to have been filed on __________ under sec.16 of the Act
- The said invention is an improvement in or modification of the invention particulars of which are given in Para-8

10. Following are the attachments with the application:

(a) Provisional specification/Complete specification
(b) Complete specification (in connection with the international application)/as amended before the International Preliminary Examination Authority (IPEA), as applicable (2 copies), No. of pages ___ No. of claims ___
(c) Drawings (in conformation with the international application)/as amended before the International Preliminary Examination Authority (IPEA), as applicable (2 copies), No. of sheets __
(d) Priority documents
(e) Translation of priority document/Specification/International Search Report
(f) Statement and undertaking on form 3
(g) Power of Authority
(h) Declaration of inventorship on Form 5
(i) Sequence listing in electronic form
(j) **Fee Rs._3500/- by** Bank Draft bearing No. 130855.Dated 25-10-2005.on STATE BANK OF PATIALA PHASE 7, MOHALI.

I/We declare that to the best of my/our knowledge, information and belief the fact and matters stated herein are correct and I/We request that a patent may be granted to me/us for the said invention.

Dated this day of November, 2005.

Signature:
Name: **Dr.Parikshit Bansal**

To,
The Controller of Patents
The Patent Office, at New Delhi

Note: *Repeat boxes in case of more than one entry
***To be signed by the applicant(s) or by authorized registered patent agent otherwise where mentioned**
***Tick (✓) / cross (x) whichever is applicable / not applicable in declaration in Para-9**
***Name of the inventor and applicant should be given in full, family name in the beginning**
***Complete address of the inventor and applicant should be given stating the postal index no./code, state and country. *Strike out the column which is/are not applicable *For fee: See First Schedule**

FORM 2

THE PATENTS ACT, 1970

(39 of 1970)

&

The Patents Rules, 2003

COMPLETE SPECIFICATIION

(See section 10 and rule 13)

IMPROVED COLUMN FOR CHROMATOGRAPHY

XYZ Institute
India

The following specification particularly describes the invention and the manner in which it is to be performed:

FIELD OF THE INVENTION

The invention pertains to the field of scientific and research devices. More specifically it pertains to an improved column for chromatography.

BACKGROUND OF THE INVENTION

Chromatography is the method of separation of molecules based on their properties e.g. charge or molecular size. The sample consisting of a mixture of molecules is passed through a column, packed with suitable matrix. Depending upon their properties, the molecules interact with the matrix with varying affinity and are released gradually, which leads to their purification/separation.

Columns available from Amersham Biosciences, USA consist of hollow, cylindrical glass tubes with a number of accessories which permit the attachment of specially designed sample applicators (Catalog, 2002. Pages 560 and 561) The overall design of the column is elaborate and complicated and does not permit volume variability of the column without the aid of specially designed 'adapter assemblies'.

Chromatography columns from Sigma-Aldrich (Catalog 2002-2003 page 2302-2303) consist of polypropylene/borosilicate tubes with fixed polypropylene end caps or threaded ends. A specially designed 'flow adapter' constructed with a PTFE eluant cannula, polyacetal body, viton O-ring seal and 20?m polyethylene bed support is combined with an open-ended column to make an adjustable bed volume column.

Chromatography columns by Amicon (Catalog 1994 publication no. 337 pg. 62) consist of cylindrical glass tubes with open, screw-threaded ends. The columns have specially designed screw-threaded adjuster assemblies, which permit variation of column volume. The columns for operational purposes, require a number of accessories viz. support net parts, plungers, nipples, connectors, screwed fittings, end cells, adjuster tubes, plunger locking and collet rings and also seals.

Similarly, Bio-Rad columns (Catalog 2002-2003 pg. 102) consist of glass tubes with screw-threaded assemblies and elaborately designed sample applicators. Different column sizes are needed for different volumes. Chromatography columns by Tosoh Bioscience, Japan have similar screw-threaded design. (Catalog, 2003 pg. 72)

Chromatography columns have been described in a number of patents also.

US patent number 6,936,166 describes an end piece for a chromatographic column, which is screw threaded. US patent numbers 6,877,363; 6,783,673; 6,736,974; 6,387,256 and 6,139,732 all describe various improvements pertaining to chromatographic columns. However, all the above columns involve use of tubes with screw threaded terminal ends or use of screw threaded supporting accessory parts. None of the columns describes a system which is totally free from screw threading of the main column tube as has been described in the present invention.

A search of the Indian, European and Australian patent databases reveals that no patent has been filed for the chromatographic column as described in present invention.

Thus, either patented or commercially available columns till date consist of screw-threaded assemblies, which require a number of accessories e.g. washers, gaskets, reducing nuts etc. Overall design of the columns is complicated and elaborate, with multiplicity of components and accessories. Moreover, they are of fixed length and different columns are needed for different sizes. For performing chromatographic separations at say three different bed heights e.g. 2 cm, 4 cm and 6 cm either 3 different columns of the required size or a specially designed adapter assembly would be needed, which would fit into a longer column and vary its length. In addition to screw-threaded assemblies, specially designed sample applicator assemblies are also needed for uniform application of the sample on the matrix.

In contrast, the present invention has a simple, compact and efficient design in which multiplicity of parts and need for accessories is altogether eliminated, owing to incorporation of a novel, multifunctional hollow bung. In existing devices as described above functions of column closure, sample application and column volume variability are performed by separate components viz. screw-threaded structures for column closing, a sample applicator assembly for uniform and efficient sample application and also a specially designed adapter assembly for varying column volume. All these components are eliminated in the present invention as the functions of column closure, sample application and variability of column volume are performed by a novel multifunctional hollow bung. By virtue of its novel design, the hollow bung serves to close the column in a totally screwless manner. Its hollow design also permits it to act as a convenient sample applicator. Being screwless, it need not be confined only to the terminal ends of column, but can be pushed down to any depth inside the column. It thus also acts as an adapter for varying column volume.

OBJECTS OF THE INVENTION

It is an object of the invention to provide a single, improved column for chromatographic separation of molecules, which permits volume variability of the matrix thus eliminating the need for columns of different sizes and also greatly reduces number of accessories needed as in existing columns.

SUMMARY OF THE INVENTION

The invention relates to an improved column for chromatography, which has a novel, screw less design, which greatly reduces the number of accessories, makes assembly simple and fast and also permits easy volume variability. The column consists of an open transparent rigid plastic tube with a fine, tapering nozzle at lower end. A novel feature of the column is a screw less, tight-fitting, hollow bung which serves to close the column simply by being pushed in from the open end. Being screw less the hollow bung need not be confined only to the terminal ends of the column and thus permits easy variability of column volume totally eliminating need of separate columns for different volumes or specially designed adapter assemblies for varying column volume. The unique hollow design of the bung, which allows entry of capillary tubing inside it also permits it to act as a convenient sample applicator, without the need for need for additional, elaborately designed sample applicator assemblies.

DESCRIPTION OF THE ACCOMPANYING DRAWINGS

Fig. 1 is a cross-sectional side view of the fully assembled column

Fig. 2 is a cross-sectional, enlarged view of the novel, multifunctional, hollow bung

DETAILED DESCRIPTION OF THE INVENTION

The invention consists of a chromatographic column which not only offers the users ease of use owing to matrix volume variability, thus eliminating the need for multiple columns, but also has greatly reduced number of accessories making operation easy and fast. Details of the column and method of working are given below:

Fig.1 illustrates the fully assembled ion-exchange chromatography column. The column consists of a hollow, transparent, rigid plastic tube **1** with upper end open and tapering nozzle **8** at lower end. Two circular glass fiber filter discs **7** are placed inside, the column at bottom. Over this, a suitable matrix **6** is gently layered. After appropriate height of matrix, a fine layer of another matrix with high porosity e.g. G-25 matrix may be layered for protection of the matrix bed. After matrix layering, column is closed by gently pushing in a screwless, tight fitting, hollow bung made of suitable flexible material e.g rubber, silicon or any other appropriate material. **3.** The bung is hollow, cylindrical, tight- fitting with an upper, closed conical top **10** and a lower, open flat circular end **11**. The hollow bung ensures an air-tight seal merely by being pushed inside the column, without the need of any screw threads. Owing to absence of screw threads, there is no need to position the rubber bung only at the terminal end. Since the bung can be conveniently pushed to any depth inside the column, height of the column is very easy to vary and different sized columns are not needed at all.

The hollow bung has wall of sufficient thickness which permits passage of sharp-ended capillary tubing **2** by puncturing and resealing. Two glass fiber discs **5** are attached to lower, circular open end **11** simply by wetting, to permit easy change whenever required. Sample application is by means of a tapering, finely pointed capillary tubing **2** which is pushed into the hollow space of the rubber bung by puncturing the thickened wall of the hollow bung from center of cone at top of bung. Capillary tubing entering the hollow bung thus acts as inlet of the column and also serves as exit point for air when the bung is pushed inside the column. The capillary tubing **2** is prevented from accidentally slipping out by incorporation of a non-return design such as flayed end of capillary tubing or by gluing a small piece of flexible silicon tubing **3** over capillary tubing.

Owing to incorporation of a hollow space inside the bung which permits entry of capillary tubing inside it and also lower open end **11** to which glass fiber discs **5** can be conveniently attached, the hollow bung acts as a convenient sample applicator. Sample application over the matrix is uniform as the inlet capillary tubing **2** reaches inside center of hollow rubber bung and the sample liquid drops exiting from the tubing fall on the glass fiber discs, thus spreading evenly and uniformly prior to entering the ion-exchange matrix **6**. This ensures efficient and uniform separation without any trailing of molecules. The hollow bung **4** thus acts as a convenient sample applicator by virtue of its design, eliminating the need for elaborately designed additional sample applicator assemblies.

The screw less design of the hollow bung enables it to take up any position inside the column, without the need for being confined only to the terminal ends of the column as is the case in screw threaded assemblies. It thus permits easy variability of column volume, totally eliminating need of separate columns for different volumes or specially designed adapter assemblies for varying column volume. The fine, tapering nozzle **8** at lower end of the column acts as the outlet to which capillary tubing can be easily and conveniently attached by a luer-lock mechanism. By utilizing a column having a partially closed end, fitted with a tapering nozzle, need for screw accessories at the outlet end of the column is eliminated.

Example : An example of the use of the device would be separation of a desired molecule from a mixture of molecules in buffer. This would involve two steps- firstly packing the column with the desired ion-exchange matrix and secondly using the packed column for separating the desired molecule from the mixture. Packing of the matrix is carried out as follows. A slurry of the appropriate matrix is prepared in buffer using a matrix:buffer ratio as recommended by the manufacturer. Slurry is then degassed under vacuum. Circular glass fiber discs of appropriate diameter are placed inside the column, covering the outlet at lower end. Degassed slurry is then poured to appropriate height in the column, after closing the outlet nozzle **8** by means of a plastic nipple. Thereafter, outlet is opened by removing nipple and degassed, filtered buffer is added continuously into the column from upper open end by means of a peristaltic pump. Washing is continued till level of gel becomes constant after which outlet 8 is again closed. A fine layer (0.5 cm) of Sephadex G-25 matrix may be layered on top of the bed to act as a bed surface protectant.

Column is then closed by gently pushing in a hollow rubber bung, till the glass fiber filter discs **5** attached to lower end of rubber bung, come to rest on top of the matrix **(Fig.1)**. Column is now ready for use. The inlet capillary tubing **2** of the column is attached to the outlet of a peristaltic pump, whose inlet takes in appropriate buffer or sample as required. Column is equilibrated by washing with appropriate buffer. Once the column is equilibrated, sample mixture is loaded onto the column through the capillary tubing **2**. Elution is carried out using a buffer containing appropriate concentration of salts and monitoring the fractions at appropriate wavelength by connecting the outlet **8** of the column to a fraction collector.

Advantages:

1. ***Easy volume variability*** - Closing of the column by means of a specially designed screw less hollow bung permits easy variability of column volume since the hollow bung being screw less need not be confined only to the terminal ends of the column. Hence, need for separate columns of different sizes or specially designed accessories for varying column volume is eliminated.
2. ***Ease of use*** - The screw less design simplifies the assembly process, making it easy and fast.
3. ***Considerably simplified, compact and efficient design*** – The compact, screwless design considerably reduces potential leakage points.
4. ***Inherent sample applicator design*** - The unique hollow design of the bung also permits it to act as a convenient sample applicator, without the need of elaborately designed accessories for sample application.
5. ***Considerable reduction in number of accessories and parts*** – Need for elaborately designed additional accessories is considerably reduced and a number of components are altogether eliminated.

We claim:

1. A column for chromatography comprising a hollow, cylindrical transparent rigid tube open at upper end, closed at the other end wherein closing of the column after matrix packing is carried out by means of a hollow bung which also helps in uniform sample application.

2. A column as claimed in claim 1 in which the lower closed end has a central finely tapered nozzle open at the tip.

3. A column as claimed in claims 1& 2 in which after packing with appropriate matrix , closing of the column is carried out by pushing in a tightly-fitting, flexible, hollow bung from the open end. The hollow bung has a conical shape, with the cone pointing upwards towards the open end, glass fiber discs at lower open flat end and finely pointed flexible capillary tubing penetrating upper conical surface of hollow bung to end into the hollow space of the bung, above surface of glass fiber filters. (Fig.2)

4. A column as claimed in claim 3 in which the hollow bung is made of suitable material e.g. silicon, rubber or any appropriate flexible material which can be inserted into the hollow tube, ensuring tight-fit and to which glass fiber discs can be attached and wherein .

5. A column of claim 3 wherein the capillary tubing entering the hollow bung acts as the inlet and the sample liquid drops exiting from the tubing fall into the hollow space of hollow bung and eventually onto the glass fiber discs, thus spreading evenly and uniformly prior to entering the matrix, ensuring efficient separation. The capillary tubing also provides an exit point for air when hollow bung is pushed down and is prevented from accidentally slipping out by a non-return type design e.g. collar attachment, flayed end/arrow headed end of capillary tubing.

6. A column of claim 1 wherein the hollow bung can be pushed to any position inside the hollow tube, thus ensuring easy and quick variability of column volume, without the need for additional accessory adapter assemblies.

7. A column of claim 1 wherein the functions of closing the column, sample application and also variability of column volume are provided by a specially designed hollow bung, which is cylindrical, flexible, tight-fitting, hollow and has a upper closed conical surface and a lower open end.

8. A column of claim 1 wherein the hollow bung has lower open end to which glass fiber disc filters are attached by means of wetting, so as to permit easy changing when desired.

9. A column of claim 1 wherein the tapering nozzle at lower end of the column acts as the outlet of the column, through which the molecules which have separated after passing through the column can be easily collected.

10. A column for chromatography as herein described with reference to the example.

Dated this .... day of ...., 2005.

Signature
Director, XXXX
(Authorized Signatory for applicant)

---

* It is important for students and researchers to understand the difference between inventor and applicant. In case a M. Pharm/ Ph.D. student comes up with a good invention and wishes to file a patent, he will sign the patent application form as an inventor and the institute will be the applicant. In case he is not attached with the institute anymore and wishes to file the patent application independently, he will sign both as inventor and applicant.

Sheet 1 of 2

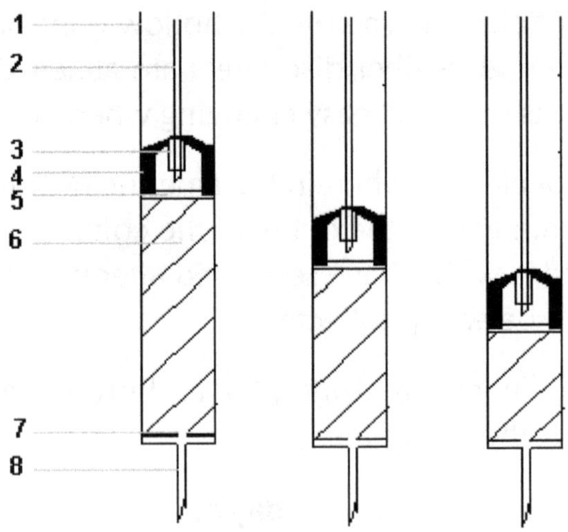

Fig. 1

Signature of applicant

Sheet 2 of 2

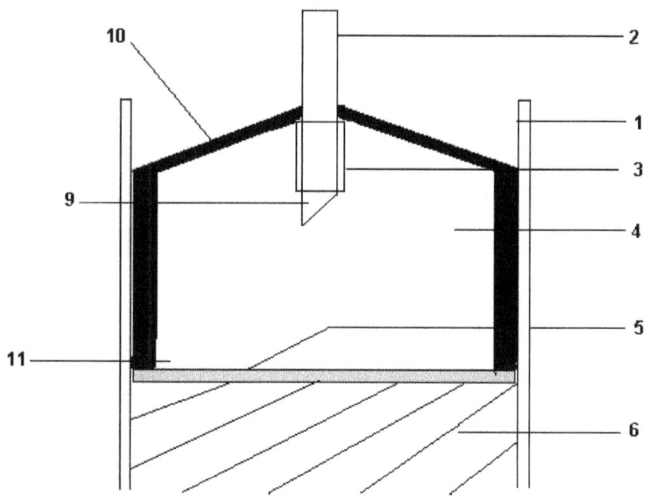

Fig. 2

Signature of applicant

ABSTRACT

The invention relates to a column for chromatography. A novel feature of the column is a mutifunctional hollow bung which totally eliminates the need for separate components and accessories for closing the column, application of sample and also varying column volume. By virtue of its novel design, the hollow bung serves to close the column in a totally screwless manner, simply by being pushed into the column. The unique hollow design of the bung, which allows entry of capillary tubing inside it also permits it to act as a convenient sample applicator, without the need for additional, elaborately designed sample applicator assemblies. Being screw less the hollow bung need not be confined only to the terminal ends of the column and thus permits easy variability of column volume, without need of separate columns for different volumes or specially designed adapter assemblies for varying column volume. The invention is simple, compact and efficient.

FORM 3

THE PATENTS ACT, 1970

(39 of 1970)

&

The Patents Rules, 2003

STATEMENT AND UNDERTAKING UNDER SECTION 8

(See section 8, rule 12)

I/We, NIPER, the applicant hereby declare -

(i) that I/We have not made any application for the same/substantially the same invention outside India – N.A.

(ii) that I/We who have made this application No.__________________ Dated __________________ alone/jointly with _________________________ made for the same/substantially same invention application(s) for patent in the other countries, the particulars of which are given below:

Name of the country	Date of Application	Application No.	Status of the application	Date of Publication	Date of Grant

(iii) that the rights in the application(s) has/have been assigned to NIPER.

(iv) that I/We undertake that upto the date of grant of the patent, by the Controller, I/We would keep him informed in writing the details regarding corresponding applications for patents filed outside India within three months from the date of filing of such application.

Dated this day of November, 2005

Applicant

To
The Controller of Patents
The Patent Office, at New Delhi

FORM 5
THE PATENTS ACT, 1970
(39 of 1970)
&
The Patents Rules, 2003
DECLARATION AS TO INVENTORSHIP
[See section 10(6) and rule 13(6)]

1. NAME OF THE APPLICANT(S) :
National Institute of Pharmaceutical Education and Research (NIPER)
hereby declare that the true and first inventor(s) of the invention disclosed in the complete specification filed in pursuance of my / our application numbered......................dated......................

2. INVENTOR(S)

1. (a) NAME	:	Dr.Parikshit Bansal
(b) NATIONALITY	:	INDIAN
(c) ADDRESS	:	Deptt. Of Pharmaceutical Technology, NIPER, Phase X, Mohali-160062

Dated this day of November, 2005

APPLICANT

3. DECLARATION TO BE GIVEN WHEN THE APPLICATION IN INDIA IS FILED BY THE APPLICANT(S) IN THE CONVENTION COUNTRY:-

We the applicant(s) in the convention country hereby declare that our right to apply for a patent in India is by way of assignment from the true and first inventor(s).

Dated this day of February, 2005

4. STATEMENT (to be signed by the additional inventor(s) not mentioned in the application form)

I/We assent to the invention referred to in the above declaration, being included in the complete specification filed in pursuance of the stated application. N.A.

Dated this _______ day of ____________________, 200____.

Signature of additional inventor(s):-
Name:-

To
The Controller of Patent
The Patent Office Branch
New Delhi

Note
*** Repeat boxes in case of more than one entry.**
*** To be signed by the applicant(s) or by authorized registered patent agent otherwise where mentioned.**
*** Name of the inventor and applicant should be given in full, family name in the beginning.**
*** Complete address of the inventor should be given stating the postal index no./code, state and country.**
*** Strike out the column which is / are not applicable.**

Form 18 is NOT to be submitted alongwith the patent application. It must be submitted after 18 months from date of submission of the patent application alongwith fee.

<table>
<tr><td>FORM 18
THE PATENTS ACT 1970
(39 of 1970)
&
The Patents Rules, 2003
APPLICATION FOR GRANT OF PATENT
[(See section 11B & rule 24B(1)(i)]</td><td>(FOR OFFICE USE ONLY)

RQ. No:
Filing Date:
Amount of Fee Paid:
CBR No:
Signature:</td></tr>
<tr><td colspan="2">1. APPLICANT (S) / OTHER INTERESTED PERSON:

(a) NAME: National Institute of Pharmaceutical Education and Research (NIPER), Mohali

(b) NATIONALITY: Indian

(c) ADDRESS: NIPER, Phase X, Mohali-160062 INDIA</td></tr>
<tr><td colspan="2">2. Statement in case of request for examination made by the applicant(s)

I/We hereby request that my/our Application for Patent No.__________________filed on ____________ for the invention titled _IMPROVED COLUMN FOR CHROMATOGRAPHY shall be examined under Sections 12 and 13 of the Act.

Or

I/We hereby make an express request that my/our application for patent No.________________filed on ____________ based on Patent Cooperation Treaty [PCT] Application No. ______________ dated ____________
made in country ____________________________________ shall be examined under sections 12 and 13 of the Act, immediately without waiting for the expiry of 31 months as specified in rule 20 (4)(ii).</td></tr>
<tr><td colspan="2">3. Statement in case of request for examination made by any other interested person

I/We the interested person request for the examination of the application no. ______________
dated ______________ filed by the Applicant ______________________ titled ______________
under sections 12 and 13 of the Act.
As an evidence of my/our interest in the application for patent following documents are submitted.

(a) ________________________________
(b) ________________________________</td></tr>
</table>

4. ADDRESS FOR SERVICE NIPER, Phase X, Mohali-160062 INDIA
Dated this day of November, 2005 To The Controller of Patent The Patent Office Branch New Delhi
NOTE: *** To be signed by the applicant(s) or by his authorized registered patent agent** *** Strike out the column which is/are not applicable**

CHAPTER-4

How should I commercialize my patent?

Filing a patent is important. But what is more important is to commercialize it! Patents filed, but not commercialized are a waste of precious human and financial resources. In this chapter, practical aspects of commercialization of patents are discussed. Concepts of Transfer of Technology (TOT) and Capture of Technology (COT) are introduced. Practical tips and suggestions are given for students for commercializing patents.

4. How should I commercialize my patent?

Patents- Important Commercial Aspects

- Granted only for products or processes- no third category.
- In India, certain categories e.g. inventions relating to atomic energy excluded
- Valid only in the countries where they are filed.
- There is no such thing as a 'world patent"
- Of fixed duration- lapse alter 20 years
- Require fee for keeping "alive"- expire if fee is not paid every year
- Can be challenged in court and got cancelled if granted wrongly

Frequently asked questions(FAQs)

1. **I have filed a patent. Why should I commercialize it?**

- Firstly, because filing and maintaining patents costs a lot of money. If you don't try to commercialize the patent, that money is being wasted.
- Secondly, patents have value only if they are commercialized. A patent filed but not commercialized is sometimes not even worth the paper on which it is printed! Remember, patents are filed only for inventions which have commercial value.
- Thirdly, it is commercialization and only commercialization which converts patents into money. Commercialization of patents leads to revenue generation for institutes and workers leading to better research facilities and opportunities. Also, financial gains for workers in terms of royalty can be considerable.
- There are ethical reasons also. Patents are usually based on research work funded by hard-earned tax payers money. If they are not commercialized, all the time and money spent on the work and also filing patents, goes waste.

2. How can I commercialize my patent?

Commercialization of a patent is quite different from filing a patent. The skills required are altogether different. However, once you understand the process, it can be quite easy. There are two ways in which you can proceed for commercialization of your patent:

1. By making efforts as an individual
2. By taking the help of some "professional' organizations also known as 'invention promotion' organizations (listed at end of this chapter) .

3. How can I as an individual make efforts to commercialize my patent?

When we talk about 'commercializing' a patent, what we mean is that we are trying to 'sell' it. locate a buyer for it. You can proceed as follows:

1. Prepare a "Technology Offer' (biodata of your invention- what? Why? How?), highlighting the main features of the invention and the benefits it offers. An illustrative format is given at end of this chapter (Annexure-1)
2. Decide on what maximum and minimum price you want to sell for and include it in the offer. If you are unable to decide just write 'price negotiable'
3. Make a list of people who can be benefit from your technology/ patent
4. Mail your tech offer to them- either through post or email
5. You can also host your tech offer in detail on the internet. Including photographs of prototypes etc. can greatly facilitate 'marketing'
6. If the buyers are not very far, fix up a personal appointment and try to meet them personally. Personal meetings and discussions can really speed up negotiations and lead to successful commercialization of a patent.

4. How can I locate buyers for my patent?

It is like asking where can I catch fish? Obviously, in the water.

Similarly, your buyers will be where the relevant industry is concentrated. If you as a pharma researcher have developed an improved process for stabilizing a formulation, just find out who are the major manufacturers of similar products, where are they concentrated. How to find this out?

- You can note down the addresses from the packaging of the existing products
- You can do a 'google' search on the internet, using relevant keywords.
- Don't rely on google alone- it is a paid search engine and prominentely shows up results of those who have paid for registration on 'google'. Try other search engines also e.g. altavista.
- Consult product catalogs
- Gather addresses from 'yellow pages" of telephone/industrial directories.
- Seek advice of professionals working in the area
- Search patent databases. They contain addresses of inventors and companies working in the relevant area in which your patent lies. They can be good buyers for your patent. Some of the free patent databases are:

1. USA	www.uspto.gov
2. European	http://ep.espacenet.com
3. Australia	www.ipaustralia.gov.au
4. Canada	http://patentsl.ic.gc.ca
5. Korea	http://www.kipris.or.kr
6. India	http://www.pfc.org.in/db/db.htm.

5. I have located the addresses of potential buyers for my inven tion. How to proceed now?

Lack of clarity or inexperience can make you lose a good buyer for your invention. Common reasons for "inventions not sold" are:

- **Pricing not clear:** Buyer tries to get minimum price and you maximum. In the process, sometimes rigidity creeps in and both turn away. Invention remains where it is - printed on paper. One way out is to remember there are not one but several ways you can satisfy mutual interests:
  - Reducing downpayment, but increasing royalty e.g. downpayment of Rs. 5 lacs and 5% royalty ,
  - Alternatively, downpayment of Rs.3 lac and royalty of 10%.
  - If buyer is still hesitant, waive off downpayment but increase royalty share to 30-40%.
  - Insert time clause e.g..agreement is valid only for 3 years or 4 years or 5 years
  - IInsert exclusivity clause e.g. ...... Rs. 20 lacs for exclusive rights for entire duration of patent or Rs.10 lac for exclusive rights for 10 years. Rs.5 lac for exclusive rights for 5 years and so on.
- **Overassessment:** Most inventors think that buyer will be able to make a profit immediately after buying an invention and overassess the value of their invention. This is not correct. Patented inventions usually need lot of investments, risks and efforts to convert them into commercially saleable products. Hence, inventor should not adopt a very rigid stand and instead be open to negotiations.

Hence, after location of buyers, getting an idea on the pricing is very important. The more buyers you can locate, greater are the chances of success and also getting a good price.

6. I contacted so many buyers for selling my patent. Indian buyers don't respond but from abroad I got a few queries. What should I do?

Don't get discouraged if local firms don't respond. Usually, if your product is such that it is not being made in India, then risk in manufacturing it in India is more and buyers may be reluctant. They may feel it is safer to just import a 'ready-to-sell' product from abroad, rather than risk money in a new invention. If a foreign firm responds, try to settle for a 'downpayment'- it may turn out to be practically very difficult for you to get royalty from abroad.

7. A foreign buyer from USA wants to know all details about my invention. I have filed patent in India only and not in USA. What should I do?

Firstly, don't panic. Even though you have not filed in USA, still you can disclose your invention to buyer by signing an NDA or 'non-disclosure-agreement'. An NDA is a legally binding agreement between buyer and seller in which it is mutually agreed that the disclosure is being made for evaluation purposes only and buyer will not commercialize the invention. NDAs usually come in standard formats and you can ask the buyer to make one. Check with a lawyer/ chartered accountant/company secretary before signing.

Secondly, it is true that if you have not filed a patent in the USA than you don't have legal rights over your invention, in USA. But neither does the buyer! In fact if you have filed a patent for your invention in India, nobody else in the world can get a patent on the same invention! Chances are that if a buyer in USA is interested in your patent, he will also try to get you to file a patent in the USA, so that monoply rights can be enjoyed by him.

8. An Indian company wants to buy my patent. They tallked about 'exclusive' rights. What does that mean?

It means that you will not sell to anyone else. Sometimes, this clause is misused- a company may buy your very good invention on exclusive basis and then deliberately not commercialize it, to prevent market of an existing product from being spoiled. You just get the downpayment. but no royalty. To avoid this, always insert a time clause in case of exclusivity' under which you indicate that if the company does not commercialize the invention in a reasonable period e.g. three years, you reserve the right to cancel the license and sell it to another person.

9. I have sold my invention. Who will bear the 'every year expenses' for maintaining the patent?

Usually the buyer, because it is his commercial interests which are being protected. Make sure it is clearly mentioned in the agreement itself, which you signed when patent was sold. If it is not mentioned, you will have to bear the expenses since you are still the owner.

10. Can I sell my patent to more than one buyer?

Yes. In that case, the agreement which you sign will be on a non-exclusive basis.

11. I feel my invention is too big for me to handle- I would like to seek the help of some professional organizations Which are the ones in India?

List of some Institutes in India assisting in Technology Transfer is given below:

1. Asia Pacific Centre for Transfer of Technology (APCTT)
   (A United Nations Institute), APCTT Building
   PO Box 4575, New Delhi-110 016 **(www.apctt.org)**

2. Technology Bureau for Small Enterprises (TBSE)

   (A Govt. of India Undertaking)

   APCTT Building, Qutab Institutional Area, PO BOX 4575

   Off New Mehrauli Road, New Delhi-110 016 **(www.techsmall.com)**

3. National Research and Development Corporation (NRDC)

   (A Govt. of India Undertaking) 20-22, Zamroodpur Community Centre, Kailash Colony Extension, New Delhi-110048 **(www.nrdcindia.com)**

4. Foundation for Innovation and Technology Transfer (FITT)

   Indian Institute of Technology, Hauz Khas, New Delhi-110016 **(fitt-iitd.org)**

   Note: FITT is an autonomous body in which Director IIT is the Chairman. Primary aim is to assist in transfer of technologies developed by IIT.

5. Grassroots Innovations Augmentation Network (GIAN)

   (National Innovation Foundation, Ahmedabad), IIT, Guwahati, Assam- 781 039

   (www.gian.org) GIAN is part of the Honey Bee Network which operates from IIM, Ahmedabad and focuses on helping inventors to 'commercialize' their technologies.

6. National Innovation Foundation (NIF)

   Bungalow no.1, Satellite Complex, Premchand Nagar Road, Jodhpur Tekra Vastrapur, Ahmedabad-380 015 **(www.nifindia.org)**

7. SRISTI **(www.sristi.org)**

   Society for Research and Initiatives for Sustainable Technologies and Institutes

8. Waterfalls Institute of Technology Transfer

   J-29, SOUTH EXTENSION PART-I, NEW DELHI-110049, India **(www.witts.org)**

9. L-RAMP **(www.lramp.org)**

   Lemelson Recognition and Mentoring Program,

   2nd Floor, IC&SR, IIT, Madras, Chennai-600036

   L-Ramp is a non-profit, voluntary organization. It is a joint initiative of IIT, Madras and the Rural Innovations Network. It is supported by the Lemelson Foundation, a private philanthropy established by a US Inventor, Jerome Lemelson and his family.

For obtaining services of a licensing specialist, a very good source is **www.lesi.org** (Licensing Executives Society Internationale) and **www.autm.org** (Association of Uninversity Technology Managers).

12. How do I select a suitable organization to help in commercialization of my patent?

See the track record. Meet and interact. Ask them how they will proceed for commercializing your invention, charges / commissions etc. Choose the one wherever you feel comfortable. But always remember- your invention is your baby. The amount of care and attention which you can give to it, nobody else can or will. Professional organizations are always there to help, but ultimately it is your enthusiasm, timely follow-ups and suitable inputs whenever you give them, which can ensure success. Remember, successful commercialization is always 'teamwork'. You must not be a 'mute' spectator.

INTRODUCTION TO TOT and COT CONCEPTS

TOT and COT are terms which most students and researchers are not likely to be familiar with. However they are very important.

Students and researchers must always remember that doing science costs a lot of money- in terms of infrastructure, chemicals and salaries. The aim of research is to benefit people, society. Research which is carried out but not transferred is research wasted. It is a huge loss of precious resources, which no country, let alone developing countries, can afford. So how to make research benefit society? The answer lies in understanding and contributing to technology dissemination. Transfer of Technology (TOT) and Capture of Technology (COT) are two approaches which every researcher must be familiar with, in case he wants his work to reach people and benefit society.

What is TOT?

It is the process by which the benefits of research are transferred to society. It can be defined as:

" Sum total of all the efforts which result in utilization of research for commercial production of goods, improvement of existing processes, development of new technologies etc.- all of which ultimately contribute to the progress and growth of society".

Though researchers, especially in developing countries are unlikely to be familiar with the concept of 'TOT', the basic steps are not difficult to understand. Once researchers grasp the concept, they can make significant contributions to TOT, not only regarding their own work, but also that of others.

Why is TOT important?

TOT is important because of several reasons:

1. **Revenue generation for institutes-** money generated is used to provide better facilities and improve infrastructure.

2. **Recognition and honour:** Immense satisfaction to researchers that what they have done has benefited people. Honour, recognitions and respect. Financial benefits.

3. **Utilization of money spent:** Most of the research being carried out in India and also other countries is in public funded institutes- our salaries and money for research comes from people. If we do not make efforts to make our research benefit society and people, it is not proper utilization of the money spent on research.

4. **Growth and development of Industry:** R&D is the backbone of industrial growth and progress. No country can compete in the global market by copying alone- new products and technologies have to be developed by original efforts.

How to carry out TOT?

- **By having a desire to ensure practical utility of your research**: The first and foremost step in TOT is to have a desire to make your research benefit society, to conduct research which has relevance and meaning.

- **By taking responsibility**: The second step is to accept that TOT does not happen by itself- someone has to make it happen. You have to spend effort and time to make your research benefit society. Perhaps it is worth spending 5-6 months on TOT of a research project on which you have spent 3-5 years of precious time and hard-earned tax-payers (parents in case of students!) money. Otherwise the work may end up in a pile of papers- of no use to anyone except you and forgotten after some time.

What are the steps involved in TOT?

Technology transfer is a well-defined process involving several steps, each of which is critical and cannot be bypassed. Based on the steps involved, a simplified model for technology transfer called 6-P model has been proposed by the author **(Fig. 4.1)**.

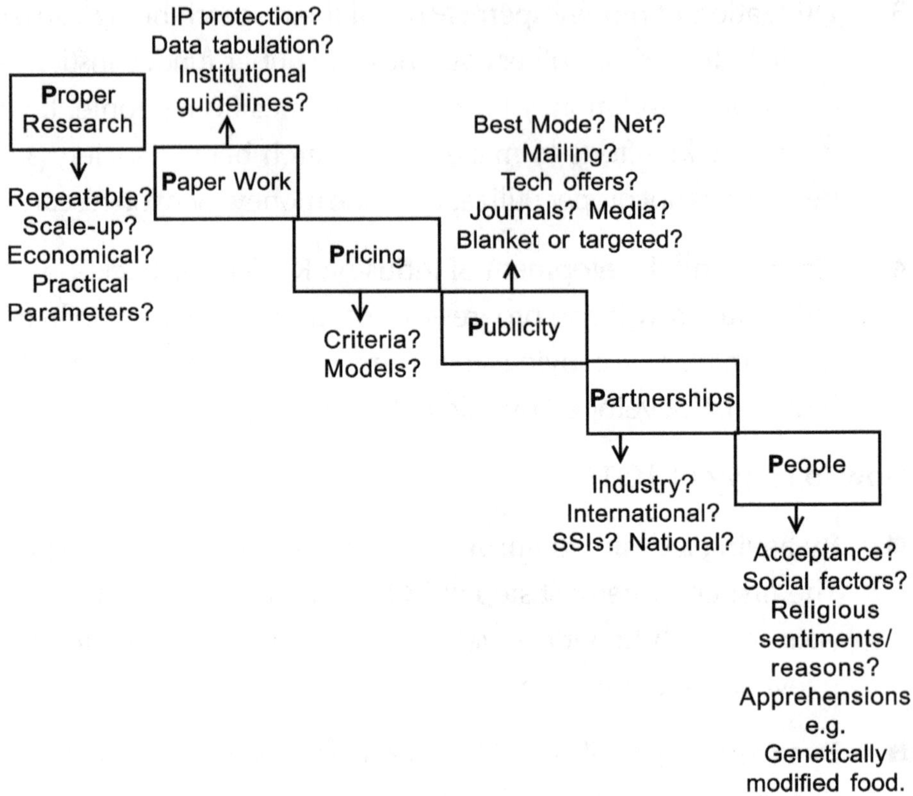

Fig. 4.1

According to this model, for successful TOT, 6 critical stages are involved:

1. **Proper Research**: By proper research, we mean firstly that in which the results are reproducible. Quite often one researcher may submit his Ph.D and when the next worker tries to repeat the work, the same is not reproducible, independently. Results at Industry level also must be capable of being reproduced. Try to address issues such as scale-up, stability etc. or other practical aspects.

2. **Paperwork**: This refers to institutional rules and guidelines regarding IP protection (patents-how to file, who will pay etc.) licensing modalities etc. which must be in place beforehand. In absence of these, decisions get delayed or mired in controversy owing to lack of fairness in decisions or fear of taking decisions e.g. case of X institute, which developed a good technology but since no guidelines were there, the researchers kept running around for two years and then gave up.

3. **Pricing**: This is the most difficult and critical area of TOT. Too high a price can put off buyers, leaving the technology unsold. Too low a price results in revenue loss. There are basically two models regarding pricing. According to one, price charged for a technology should depend upon market forces i.e. impact of the technology irrespective of amount spent on developing it. The second model proposes that price charged should include all expenses involved in developing it. Irrespective of the model followed for pricing, it is important to decide the price beforehand- you cannot sell anything without fixing its price first. Negotiations are always there but a minimum figure has to be decided prior to that.

4. **Publicity**: You have done wonderful research, but who will buy your technology if nobody knows about it? How to go about publicity is an important and critical step in TOT. Also, in case of technology blanket publicity e.g. mass mailing to industry does not work. Why would a manufacturer of eye-drops be interested in information about a new cardiovascular drug you have developed? He would be more interested in a technology for stabilizing eye-drops. On the other hand, a manufacturer of cardiovascular medicines will not be interested about your

technology for stabilizing eye-drops. It is important to identify and then approach buyers ie.adopt targeted publicity and not blanket publicity. Specific journals, websites, letters to manufacturers, personal selective visits etc. are some commonsense approaches which can help in locating buyers.

5. **Partnerships**: This means working alongwith industry. If an industry approaches you for getting rights to use your research work, you should have at least some idea of what will be involved. Signing of documents (Confidentiality Agreements, Material Transfer Agreements (MTAs) and a detailed MOU or Memorandum of Understanding are the fundamental steps involved. In addition, critical technical inputs may be needed from your end for successful uptake of the technology developed by you or your technology may get a tag of 'failed technology'. So, understand the value of 'partnering' with industry, as a researcher.

6. **People's acceptance**: It is no use trying to develop a technology which people will not accept e.g. due to religious reasons/social concerns etc. It will be a sheer wastage of resources if after spending years of research and other aspects, a technology fails at last stage because people's acceptance had not been taken into consideration. Or maybe the concerns in minds of people had not been addressed during the course of development of the technology e.g. genetically modified food, irradiated vegetables, processed beef in India, improved capsules made of non-vegetarian material , use of cows for ploughing fields (religious sentiments of people in some countries, may not allow acceptance of this, no matter what the scientific data says) etc.

Technology Offers- Biodatas of your research work

Every student is familiar with use of the terms " CV" or " Bio-Data" or " Resume". To get placements after completing their studies, students put in considerable time and effort to design and write a beautiful and impressive CV. It is natural- every student feels he has put in considerable effort and money to earn his degree and must be 'placed' with a suitable employer, so that he can start contributing and also earning!.

But what about the 'research work' done by researchers? Even that needs 'placement'. For this, students must be familiar with how to write 'biodatas' of their research work so that Industry can be contacted easily and 'placements' of their work also occur.

A Technology Offer is the 'biodata' of an invention/research work. Just as a precise and well-written biodata of a candidate attracts employers, so also a well-written 'technology offer' will attract buyers.

What does a technology offer consist of ? How to write it? It is not at all difficult! In fact, almost all researchers may feel confident after seeing the formats of two technology offers, given below.

Just as in a personal biodata, headings are more or less standard, so also in a 'technology offer'. The headings given in the sample formats below are suggestive, but quite practical. They enable a buyer to quickly judge whether he is interested in your work or not.

Formats of some more technology offers can be explored by students, by using the keywords 'technology offers' and searching using a search engine e.g. google, altavista or any other. A good site for viewing actual technology offers is www.apctt.org.

Formats of two technology offers are given below and are quite illustrative:

TECHNOLOGY OFFER-1

A NON-INFRINGING PROCESS FOR THE MANUFACTURE OF OCTYL-METHYL-CINNAMATE (OMC)

XYZ Institute, a leading institute in Pharmaceutical Research offers a novel, non-infringing process for the manufacture of OMC, which is the main component of sunscreen lotions and creams (cosmetic products). The process involves use of an environment friendly method, which essentially consists of a metal catalyzed reaction in a cheap ionic liquid. The catalyst and ionic liquid can be recycled several times. The global requirement of this product is more than 5000 metric tons/annum.

Areas of application

Cosmetics (Sunscreen lotions/creams)

Advantages of the technology

1. Single step reaction
2. Easily available raw materials
3. No environmental pollution. Catalysts and solvents are recyclable.
4. Clean production and convenient operation
5. Non-infringing new process. No violation of patents of existing companies.

Stage of Development

Proven at Laboratory scale. Scale-up to be done. Facilities for scale-up exist at Institute (Pilot plant available).

IP Status

Novel process. Patent for the same already filed by the institute.

Economic Data

Prevailing market price of the major manufacturer (BASF) is approximately ABC per /Kg. Estimated production cost as per this process is much lower.

Transfer Forms

Technology licensing and know-how

Licensing Fee

Negotiable.

Contact Person

(You can give your own name, name of your guide/supervisor or any duly authorized person designated as per rules of your institute/organization)

TECHNOLOGY OFFER-2

A NOVEL, NON-INFRINGING PROCESS FOR THE MANUFACTURE OF LEVOBUPIVACAINE

XYZ INSTITUTE, , a leading institute in Pharmaceutical Research offers a novel, non-infringing process for the manufacture of an improved widely used local anesthetic, Levobupivacaine. The process uses a chiral catalyst for asymmetric synthesis of the product.

Areas of application

Local anesthetic product. Widely used in hospitals in surgical/gynecological procedures.

Advantages of the technology

1. Uses easily available raw materials.
2. Faster compared to existing process as no resolution involved.
3. Cheaper as use of expensive resolving agents is altogether eliminated.
4. Non-infringing new process. No violation of patents of existing companies.

Stage of Development

Proven at Laboratory scale. Scale-up to be done. Facilities for scale-up exist at Institute (Pilot plant available).

IP Status

Novel process. Patent for the same already filed by the institute.

Economic Data

Commercially the product is known as Chirocaine and is already approved for clinical use. Regarded as superior to other local anesthetics owing to lesser side products. NO MANU FACTURER IN INDIA YET.

Transfer Forms

Technology licensing and know-how

Licensing Fee

Negotiable.

Contact Person

(You can give your own name, name of your guide/supervisor or any duly authorized person designated as per rules of your institute/organization)

From the brief introduction about TOT as given above, it must be clear that Technology Transfer is an important activity for researchers.

In developed countries, the concept of having dedicated departments or offices for technology transfer is well-known. Most of the Universities and Research Institutes in the United States have either an Office of Transfer of Technology and Licensing or have tie-ups with specialized organizations for commercialization of research.

However, for developing countries which are in the initial stages of grasping the fundamentals of IPRs, having such dedicated offices is still a faraway dream! Financial resources, infrastructure and trained human resources for bringing about TOT impose tough challenges which not many countries may be able to overcome easily.

In this context a new concept proposed by me, COT or Capture of Technology, may offer a practical low-cost alternative which developing countries might find easier to promote and adopt. It avoids the need for setting up dedicated departments/offices or employing trained human resources for Technology Transfer purposes, in Universities or Research Institutes. Instead, it aims at setting up of dedicated IPR and Technology Cells in the Industry, for which expenses are borne by industry.

COT- A new concept for helping in research utilization

Intellectual Property Rights (IPRs) and Transfer of Technology (TOT) are two facets of knowledge which are critical in making any industry globally competitive. Unfortunately, developing countries have a long way to go in both areas. IPRs and technology management as a compulsory subject is yet to be introduced in the course curriculum, at PG level in most technical institutes in developing countries, including India. As a result, professionals emerging from these institutes are not IP and technology transfer savvy. Also, hardly any institute has dedicated TOT professionals, who help in transfer of technology

(TOT). The result is lots of patents filed, but not commercialized! Getting trained professionals in the area of IPRs and also TOT poses a challenging task. How to overcome the problem? The answer lies in a new concept viz. Capture of Technology (COT).

Why TOT is difficult in the context of developing countries?

1. **Lack of trained human resources**: Technology transfer is a specialized area requiring people not only with technical skills, but also additional skills related to IPRs, technology management, technology pricing, publicity, etc. Since TOT as a subject is yet to gain importance or acceptance in most developing countries including India, getting people who can contribute to TOT becomes very difficult for institutes.

2. **Lack of focus**: Even now, primary focus of funding agencies and also institutes is to carry out more and more research, resulting in more and more publications, but not actual utilization of research. TOT as an area of focus is surprisingly missing! Projects are given readily for research, but rarely one comes across a project aiming at commercialization of research already carried out! Scholarships and financial aid by funding agencies is targeted towards supporting research but not promoting the actual use and commercialization of research for the benefit of society.

3. **Cumbersome process**: Technology transfer as a process is quite cumbersome. It involves 6 well defined steps viz. proper research, paperwork, pricing, publicity, partnerships and people's acceptance, each of which is critical and cannot be bypassed. In the absence of TOT awareness, the link breaks at one point or the other, resulting is abandoning of efforts.

4. **Lack of motivation**: In absence of well-defined policies for sharing of financial benefits between funding organizations, institutes and inventors, there is lack of motivation amongst researchers to put

in efforts for commercializing their research. Also, promotional policies etc. bank heavily on number of publications (and also to some extent patents), but not on technologies commercialized. If a worker makes efforts to commercialize his work, he may do so at the cost of publications, resulting in career losses.

5. **Absence of industry partnerships**: Research project proposals rarely have experts from industry. Institutes have placement cells for students, but not for 'placements' of their work/technologies for which considerable inputs of time, money and effort have gone in! Networking with industry in a well-defined co-ordinated manner (similar to dedicated placement cells for students) is essential for TOT, which is missing in most institutes.

***

COT- How it Differs from TOT

TOT and COT are just two sides of the same coin- strategies to enable research to benefit society! A comparison of both is given in Table 4.1 below:

Table 4.1 TOT vs COT.

Parameter	Transfer of Technology (TOT)	Capture of Technology (COT)
1. Stage of initiation	At level of academic institute	At level of industry
2. Speed of execution	Determined by institute policies, availability of manpower etc. Slow.	Much faster as decision making is at level of industry.
3. Motivation level of personnel	Low. Promotional policies lay emphasis on number of publications and not on technologies actually commercialized.	High, since technological superiority is directly related to market advantages and profits.
4. Operation	Long and cumbersome process, involving decision making in academic/govt. institutes. Invariably gets bogged down at one step or the other.	Swift process, unlikely to get bogged down at level of industry, since direct advantages and profits are involved.
5. Direction of Movement	From institute to Industry	From industry to institute
6. Scope	Limited to technologies from a particular institute involved in the TOT process.	Very broad and not restricted to any one institute. Under COT, industry tries to source technologies from multiple sources, not only within the country but also abroad.
7. Strength Recognition	TOT recognizes and gives importance to R&D work carried out by research institutes. It then looks for suitable partners in industry to take up and commercialize the work.	COT recognizes and gives importance to manufacturing set-ups. It is is based on the recognition that no matter how good a technology generated by an institute is, it will not benefit the country, if a manufacturing set-up is not there.

COT- What is it?

" It is the process by which an industry is able to get hold or 'capture' a technology from an external source, which may be a public funded research institute or another Industry, situated within the country or abroad."

COT- How does it occur?

COT occurs by linking together two distinct groups – Knowledge creators and Knowledge users. It is based on the recognition that these are the two well-defined groups in the technology development and utilization process (Fig. 4.2).

Knowledge creators are Academic/Research institutes e.g. . NIPER, IMTECH, PGI, CSIO (Chandigarh) IISC (Bangalore), CCMB (Hyderabad), Universities etc. These are Public Funded and heavily dependent on grants and government. (People's) money. They are not involved in any manufacturing or sale activity and do not produce any goods. They create knowledge through research activities e.g. M.Sc/Ph.D Thesis, publications, books etc. but DO NOT use this knowledge for the manufacture of goods.

Knowledge users, on the other hand are industries e.g. Pharma, engineering, chemicals, electronics, food processing, etc . Unlike govt./academic institutes these are self-funded, relying on profits from manufacturing and sales activities. They hardly create knowledge in the contemporary sense. Rather, they are 'knowledge users' utilizing the inputs from R&D of "knowledge creators" to standardize and carry out well-defined production processes.

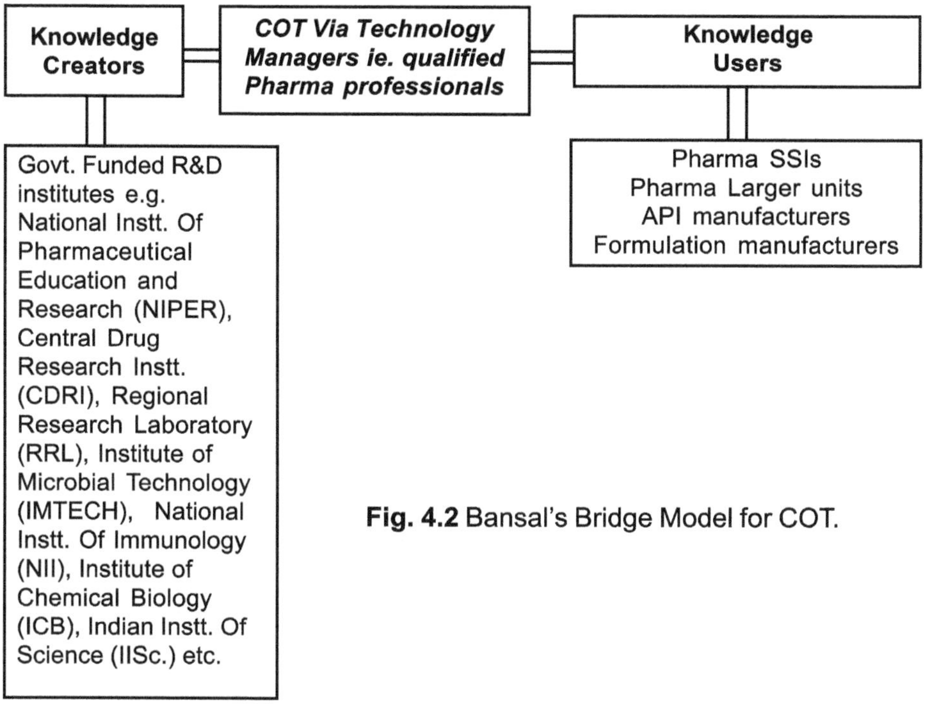

Fig. 4.2 Bansal's Bridge Model for COT.

COT offers a practical, well-defined strategy for linking the two, so that industry can enjoy the benefits of 100% R&D at virtually zero cost.

COT – Mechanism of operation

In TOT, the strategy involved for promoting dissemination of technology is to set-up a Technology Transfer Cell within the institute. Some institutes call it Office of Technology Licensing. The cell requires trained personnel and permanent inflow of funds to maintain it. In contrast, COT involves training of industry personnel in sourcing of technology, in a professional and dedicated manner. Once an industry is able to appreciate that it can get virtually 100% benefits of research at zero cost, COT becomes a very powerful incentive on part of industry to remain alert to technological advances and grab them as soon as they become available.

For COT, industry has to take certain basic steps, which can enable it to make use of research benefits offered by R&D conducted in public funded institutes. The institutes also stand to gain by COT, since the activity will result in revenue generation by way of lumpsum payments and royalties from industry.

Mechanism of operation is very simple and as follows:

1. **Creation of a Technology Cell**: Set up a dedicated 'Technology Cell' within the industry and appoint a 'Technology Manager in this cell. Technology Manager is an existing employee or a newly appointed person with a technical background.

2. **MOUs**: Sign Memorandum of Understanding (MOUs) with institutes working in your area of interest e.g. in case of Pharma industry, MOUs with, Pharma Deptts. of Universities / Research Institutes etc. can be useful. MOUs simply put are 'agreements with a legal binding'. MOUs should be focused in nature indicating clearly that the industry is willing to help the institute in commercialization of its R&D work and also offer its facilities for scale-up and trials. In return, institute is willing to take up joint projects with industry. Spelling out the royalty benefits in the MOU itself e.g. 5% on net sales for a specified period e.g. 5-7 years, in case any technology from institute is commercialized, helps to avoid delays and complications at later stages. The advantage of this to industry is that it can simultaneously network with several institutes all over a country and thus give / receive inputs in several areas. Working individually, an industry would find it very difficult to maintain a research profile spanning several areas. However through COT it can easily interface with institutes working in different areas of commercial interest to the industry.

3. **Linkages with TOT institutes**: Registering one's compay with institutes involved in TOT e.g. in India, the following institutes

can be useful: Asia Pacific Centre for Transfer of Technology (APCTT), New Delhi, National Research and Development Corporation (NRDC), New Delhi etc. is a powerful method of getting hold of the latest technologies . (Addresses/website links at Annexure-1)

4. **Regular search of Patent Databases:** Patent databases are a powerful source of Industrially useful information, which is available FREE OF COST. Some of the useful websites are given in annexure 2. For an industry, it is not possible to read and subscribe to journals, which can be many and may not carry commercially important information . In contrast, patent database is ONLY ONE per country . Regular reading and search of patent databases is a powerful method for COT.

Advantages of using patent databases as tools in COT:

a. Identification of new and emerging technologies

b. Identification of suitable technology partners at national/ international level

c. Monitoring of global technology trends

d. Facilitation of global trade by adoption of non-infringing processes or licensing of available inventions/innovations

e. Protection of existing business by being alert to new technological developments, which can lead to fall in product price of existing products or lead to better and improved products, thus affecting market of existing products. COT thus acts as a 'defence'

COT Concept testing

Based on personal interaction with selected Industry professionals in India, the author realized that awareness on IPRs and

Technology aspects was very low. Hence, if awareness regarding practical aspects of IPRs and Technology sourcing could be created amongst industry professionals, it could be a powerful tool in helping in technology dissemination, by enabling industry to go in for COT.

To test the concept, the author discussed COT with a leading industrial house. The response was immediate. The management within a week ensured follow-ups, created a separate cell and sought guidance for its existing staff to make use of the concept. The industrial house realized the blunder it was making by investing heavily in R&D, without being aware of the global technological advances and also technological generation within the country. It realized the powerful impact COT could make in its profits, global competitiveness and also product/process improvement. It realized that not only did it have to make dedicated efforts to know the latest technological innovations taking place, it also needed to have well-defined mechanisms to get hold of the technological innovations. That essentially is the essence of COT.

This was in sharp contrast to TOT, where repeated efforts made by the author at various stages in different academic and research institutes, had met with complete failure. The moment questions of policy level decisions came in to execute the process, the TOT process got jammed. The author feels executing the TOT process in government and public funded institutes is an exercise in futility, especially in developing countries! It involves too many policy level decisions, which nobody feels comfortable with. Moreover, the motivation is never strong enough. Creating separate cells or departments in public funded institutes is a herculean task. Existing staff when burdened with additional duties of TOT is never able to do justice to the work. However, the moment the focus is shifted to industry, the motivation is very high- because direct profits are involved. Decisions making is rapid and the support for technology 'capture' is tremendous.

Concluding remarks

Transfer of technology does not happen by itself. Somebody has to make it happen. It needs trained resource people at level of Universities and Academic Institutes- a practical problem in the context of developing countries. COT which aims at utilizing existing manpower in Industry offers a practical and easier option for technology dissemination. The concept is important for industry, as it enables the industry (Knowledge user) to overcome its lack of R&D infrastructure handicap while for academic and research institutes (Knowledge creators) the concept offers attractive incentives for resource generation and better facilities for researchers, by way of royalties for technologies licensed out to industry. The concept of COT is timely as there is increasing pressure on R&D institutes to generate their own resources and also go in for commercialization of research/patents which institutes have filed. It is important for professionals from science and technology streams to understand and make use of COT as most of them will be joining the industry and very few will pursue academics.

Practice Questions:

1. What strategy will you as a researcher adopt to commercialize your research work?

2. Prepare technology offer of your M.Pharm/Ph.D work.

CHAPTER-5

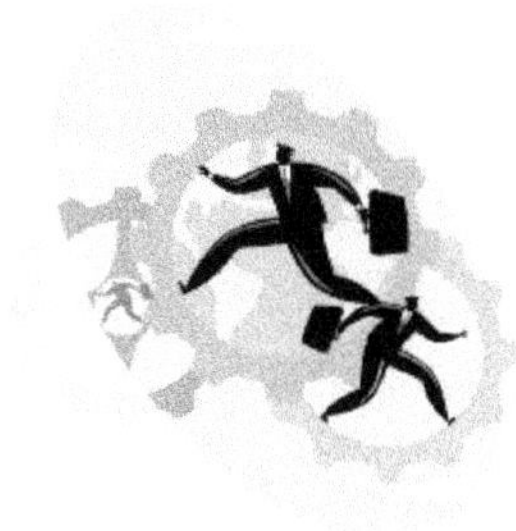

How can I integrate IPRs into my research work?

The knowledge of IPRs is not merely theoretical, but very applied and practical, provided one understands and makes use of it. In this chapter, a 'workable strategy' for integration of IPRs and technology management into research, by students and researchers is discussed.

5. How can I integrate IPRs into my research work?

Simply knowing about IPRs, patents and searching alone does not lead to their practical utilization by researchers. Searching patent databases on regular basis, reading all the patents which come up in the search and utilizing them on a practical basis to improve the quality of research requires a lot of effort and patience.

Why to integrate IPRs into research?

The benefits of integrating knowledge of IPRs , especially searching patent databases and compiling the information have already been discussed in the earlier chapters but are reproduced again for convenience:

1. **Avoiding duplication:** of R&D work (patented work is quite often not published in journals)
2. **Global overview:** Knowing GLOBAL TECHNOLOGY STATUS of the area in which you are working (where is the world standing in what you are doing?)
3. **Avoiding infringements:** Your entire project can go waste, if AFTER COMPLETION you find that you cannot commercialize it because it violates someone else's patent.
4. **Buyer identification:** You will come to know which companies might be interested in your research work (collaborations, sponsorship, funding or even in buying your patents!)
5. **Identification of patentability value of your work:** You will yourself be able to pin-point whether you can patent your work or not!

6. **Employer identification:** For Ph.D students, integration of IPRs into their research work can be a powerful tool in identification of prospective employers. Names of the company/institutes working in related areas are given in the patents.

How to integrate IPRs into your Ph.D work?

Some practical, easy to implement steps are given below:

1. **Regularity:** Patent applications are published on a weekly basis. Fix any one day in a week e.g. Friday.

   - Regularly scan worldwide patent databases.
   - Download the patents and save them in a folder for detailed reading later.
   - Take printouts of the relevant patents
   - Put hard copies in a properly labelled file e.g. patents on curcumin or patents on curcumin manufacturing process etc.

2. **Search patent applications ALSO and not the granted patents alone:** A very common mistake made by researchers is that they search GRANTED patents, forgetting that even patent applications which are already filed are important. Their entire work can go waste, if somebody has already filed an application!

   - If searching the USPTO site, visit the 'patent applications' site also.
   - Grant of a patent takes around 3 years. If you restrict your search to only granted patents, you are behind by 3 years!!

3. **Special precaution in case of Indian Patent Databases:** Indian patent database as such is not available on the internet. The patent office journals have to be downloaded every week and can then be searched digitally, offline. Hence, it is very important

that Ph.D students make it a regular habit to download the journal every week. Failing this, they may end up duplicating work or not knowing which company has entered into India. Even otherwise, if an Indian company wants to license in the Ph.D work for use in India, it is the Indian Patents which matter and not the foreign filings!

4. **Getting full-text of Indian patents relevant to your research work:** Unfortunately, unlike European and US sites, where the full patents can be downloaded, in case of Indian Patents, the full-text is not available online. These have to be ordered from the respective patent office brances. Hence, after knowing which patents are of interest, a researcher must keep track of the same and order full-text of the patents. It is only after reading the full-text of the patents, can one know whether the Ph.D work one is doing is really new or it is 'already disclosed' in the patent.

5. **Information compilation and retrieval:** Ensure that you maintain a file in which you regularly enter data on searches carried out, keywords used and also results obtained. Hard copies are preferrable.

6. **Patent filing:** Once you are regularly monitoring patents, you at once come to know whether any innovation in your work/lab is patentable or not. If yes, just go ahead and file a provisional application. DO NOT WAIT for all data to be generated! Not many countries allow filing of a provisional patent application-USA and India do. Go ahead and take advantage.

7. **Have the templates ready:** Maintain a folder of 'Forms' which have to be used for filing a patent. It facilitates filing, whether done through IPR cell of your institute or through your patent attorney. Be familiar with basic elements of drafting a patent application.

8. **Know what's going on in the market:** Search out the potential buyers of your research from patent databases and actual interactions with possible buyers. Find out competing products in market- carry out cost comparisons, get suggestions from industry. Your experiments may end up getting redesigned!

   - Visit www.apctt.org regularly

9. **Be clear of institutional policies and rules:** Get a copy and keep for reference. You must be clear what forms to fill, how to fill them and what permission to seek.

Caution!

Most students review only literature when preparing their synopsis. This is a mistake! A practical approach can be to prepare a review, based not only on literature, but under three heads as follows:

Review:

1. Review of Literature

2. Review of Patents and patent applications

3. Review of Commercial information (pertaining to the proposed research work) e.g. if proposing a project on a new process, review of commercial information on existing processes being acutally used in Industry can add value to the research project. For a new product, interaction with manufacturers, review of company catalogs, brochures, websites etc. can be illuminating!

   Thus, an M.Pharm or a Ph.D thesis can truly become useful if such an approach is adopted.

Practice Questions/activity

1. What steps will you take to ensure that duplication of your research work is not occuring / will not occur?
2. How will you check on the status of Indian Patent Applications?
3. Why review of literature alone is not sufficient when proposing a research project?

CHAPTER-6

Why are ethics important in IPRs?

The knowledge of IPRs is not merely theoretical, but very applied and practical. Owing to confidential nature of information being disclosed, it becomes imperative for IPR professionals to maintain a high standard of ethics and values, so that the trust reposed in them by inventors is not violated.

6. Why are ethics important in IPRs?

The knowledge of IPRs is a very specialized one. Owing to the confidential nature of information which is disclosed to IP professionals, it is of critical importance that IP professionals practice good ethics and avoid misuse of trust imposed in them by inventors. In the present lecture, the importance of ethics and values for professionals is discussed.

Importance of Ethics for Professionals

Ethics and values give strength to individuals, to society and to a country. They keep society intact. In absence of ethics, society and eventually countries can break up. It is individuals which make a society, a country. Weak and bad individuals cannot make a strong country, a strong nation. A society becomes good or bad based on the ethical values of individuals.

Ethics and values are very important in case of professionals e.g. medical, research, pharma, legal etc. This is because personal decisions affect us and our family, but professional decisions have far reaching consequences as they affect the entire society. Hence, it is very important that they should be correct. What is the benchmark for correct decisions? The benchmark is ethics. Ethics contribute to right decision making. When our value system is clear, it becomes a lot easier to make correct decisions and commitments.

In modern times, with so many personal and professional challenges, it is all the more important to develop a strong sense of ethics. This is because ethics and values are the lighthouse which guide us in the turbulent sea of life. A person without a sense of ethics and values is a lost person, unable to decide what is wrong and what is right.

Questions and answers

1. Are ethics and values obsolete?

No, they can never be obsolete. We live in modern times- in an age of internet, computers, jets, advanced medical care and so many other things. We live in an age where everything is fast, including food! We may at times wonder- perhaps ethics and values are obsolete. This is not true- no matter how modern and advanced we become, values never go out of fashion. e.g.

- **Honesty** (doing the right thing, even if nobody is watching)
- **Integrity** (being able to generate trust in people on account of fair dealing)
- **Fairness** (taking decisions based on merit, without being influenced by prejudice)
- **Compassion** (being a good human first and a good professional afterwards) e.g. a doctor may be very good as a professional, but if he is rude to the patients it will not help them.

These values are always respected, no matter where you are, how modern you are.

2. Are ethics and values relative i.e. varying from person to person, country to country?

No, ethics and values are never relative. They are universal just like the laws of gravity. They are the golden standards which determine our quality as individuals, as professionals, as humans. These standards are the same throughout the world just as 1 Kg of salt is 1kg whether in India, USA or UK. Bad circumstances are no excuses for making bad choices-just because you don't have money, does not give you the right to steal. Values and ethics are not just designed for good times, but also to prevent bad times. They are like the laws of land- needed when people are good, but badly needed when people turn bad!

3. Do ethics have any role in our business/professional lives?

Yes, they do. In fact they are all the more important in business and professional life because of the large number of interactions which take place when one becomes a professional. A professional without ethics can hurt many, can hurt society badly. Ethics or lack of it is evident in every profession. Greedy doctors indulge in unfair practices-commissions on prescriptions of inferior medicines, recommending avoidable investigations or even doing unnecessary procedures and surgery. Lawyers bend the truth. Parents and children alike tell white lies. Accountants and secretaries falsify reports. Superiors instead of taking the blame, punish subordinates. When we cheat the people around us, we not only cheat ourselves, but also prepare to get cheated. Professional achievements bring responsibility. We cannot build industry and infrastructure while destroying moral and social fiber.

4. What affects ethics?

Greed, Fear, Pressure (GFP)

Greed

Greed is primarily for money, for power. But sometimes when we compromise our values and ethics to get these, we realize the value of not what we have got, but what we have lost.

The story of king Midas beautifully illustrates this.

King Midas loved gold, he was really greedy for it. Once when god asked him to wish for anything he wanted, he wished that anything he touched, be changed to gold. His wish was granted. His bed, clothes anything he touched became gold. His happiness knew no bounds! But then something strange happened. He could not eat or drink! His food, water changed to gold, the moment he touched it. He was hungry. He saw his daughter and hugged her- she became a statue! He cried- because he got what he wanted but lost everything!

He begged god for forgiveness and was very happy when whatever he touched became normal. He realized gold (money!) was not everything in life. We may compromise a lot for money, but in the end may realize that we have lost more, because we did not realize its value.

Fear

This is also another factor contributing to loss of ethics- fear of losing a job, being victimized or being left behind. But sometimes its worth stopping and asking yourself — Is the fear really worth that much? What is the worse that can happen? How to overcome your fears?

- Speaking out and sharing your fears with people close to you viz. friends, family members can be a great help in overcoming them.
- Emotions kept inside tend to gather negative thoughts. They can become big enough to affect your health, professional performance, decisions and judgements.
- Be bold, share your thoughts, seek help.
- Believe in yourself.
- Do not compromise on your ethics- you will open the door to more fears.

Pressure

Modern living is full of pressure. Pressure clouds judgement and clear thinking, leading to ethics and values being compromised- fudging of data to meet deadlines, signing papers without reading, passing judgements without understanding etc. Do not deny but accept that pressure exists and find ways to deal with it. Since it is we who are affected, it is up to us to find a solution. Some practical solutions are:-

- Learning to plan and maintain a diary
- Developing a habit to read and keep yourself informed
- Develop and maintain a hobby
- Learn meditation/yoga or whatever suits you.

Remember, personal happiness is very important. Do not allow your professional life to suffocate everything – keep time for yourself. KEEP A HOBBY ALIVE. It is worth it.

5. Where do we get our values and ethics from?

We get our degrees from schools, colleges but where do we get our values and ethics from? Are they taught? This is a question which each of us has to answer himself or herself. Maybe it is schools, teachers or family/parents. Maybe it is religion. But whatever it is, it affects life- yours and of those around you. Learn to value ethics. Identify your source of values and strengthen it- maybe it is reading a prayer book, visiting and interacting with someone whom you regard as your guide or just thinking and reflecting (meditation?). Life is never smooth- at times it can be very rough. Those are the times when you need strength. Values and ethics give you strength- from within.
An exhaustive list of various sources of ethics listed by students in response to a questionnaire by author is given in annexure-1. A study by Reader Digest (April 1996) beautifully illustrates various facets of ethics. Results of the study are summarized in Annexure-2.

Conclusion

The foundations of any good business or professional achievement rest on good values and ethics. Weak and corrupt individuals do not make strong nations. Quite often we tend to give too much value to negativity, forgetting all that is positive and beautiful around us.

Practice Questions:

1. What is the source of your ethics and values?
2. Narrate any one personal incident which strengthened your sense of ethics.
3. Supposing you join at a senior level managerial position in a pharma company. What practical steps will you take to inculcate a sense of ethics and values at your workplace?

Annexure-1

Table 1: Source of ethics and values

S. No.	Source	% of students indicating this parameter*
1.	Family (Parents and grandparents)	98%
2.	Teachers	92%
3.	Religion/Epics	80%
4.	Books, Novels	70%
5.	Famous Personalities/Public figures	30%
6.	Friends	30%
7.	Life (personal experiences)	10%
8.	Movies	10%
9.	Organization where one works	5%
10.	Spouse	1%
11.	Past life	1%

* Pooled data based on responses of M.Pharm./MBA (Pharm.) students (n = 266) at National Institute of Pharmaceutical Education and Research (NIPER), Mohali, INDIA (Years 2004-2006).

Annexure-2

A study by Reader's Digest (April, 1996) beautifully illustrates the concept of ethics and values.

WALLET TEST

A Reader's Digest Team 'loses' a purse containing $50, with address and phone no. in 12 cities across America. 10 purses are lost in each city. Aim is to find out 'how honest are americans'.

Questions:

1. Are people nowadays dishonest?
2. Are people in small cities more honest?
3. Who is likely to be more honest- males or females?
4. Are young peoples less likely to be honest than adults?
5. What is the source of Values

Results

Big Cities	**Returned**	**Kept**	
Seattle	9	1	
St.Louis	7	3	
Atlanta	5	5	
Average	70%		
Suburbs	Returned	Kept	
Los Angeles	6	4	
Houston	5	5	
Boston	7	3	
		Average	**60%**
Medium Cities	**Returned**	**Kept**	
Greensboro, N.C.	73		
Las Vegas	5	5	
Dayton, Ohio	5	5	
		Average	**57%**

Small Towns	Returned	Kept
Meadville, Pa	8	2
Concord, NH	8	2
Cheyenne, Wyo	8	2
		Average 80%

Answers

- **Are people nowadays dishonest?**
  No, more than 50% people still returned the purses and were honest. In some cities there was remarkable figure of 90% even. Overall average was 67%.

- **Are people in small cities more honest?**
  Apparently. Score for the smaller cities-80%.

- **Who is likely to be more honest- males or females?**
  Females-72% returned the purse vs 62% males

- **Are young peoples less likely to be honest than adults?**
  No, 10 of the 15 people encountered returned the purse, indicating youngsters are trustworthy (67% average).

- **What is the source of Values?**
  Parents, teachers, religion and just being human-desire to help each other. Makes you feel good.

CHAPTER-7

What are the important IPR related treaties and international agreements I should be aware of as a Pharma student/ researcher?

In this chapter, important international treaties and agreements which a pharma professional should be aware of, are discussed and explained. GATT/TRIPS and WTO, DOHA DECLARATION (including data exclusivity concepts) and HATCH-WAXMAN ACT.

7. What are the important IPR related treaties and international agreements I should be aware of as a Pharm student researcher?

7.1 GATT/TRIPS Agreement and WTO

7.2 DOHA Declaration (including Compulsory Licensing & Data Exclusivity concepts)

7.3 Hatch-Waxman Act

7.1 GATT/TRIPS AGREEMENT AND WTO — BASIC CONCEPTS

An important aspect of IPRs is their power to influence Trade. Two well-known cases in the Indian context are the patents for Basmati Rice and Haldi filed in the US which were bitterly opposed by India, as these affected exports. Patent laws were recently amended in India to bring them in harmony with International regulations. Not only India, but several countries worldwide also modified their patent laws to bring them in harmony with common laws accepted under International Agreements. What was the need to change laws in different countries? What are the benefits to Industry? The answer to these questions lie in history when GATT was born and in the present when GATT has matured into an adult, the WTO.

GATT *(General Agreement on Tariffs and Trade)* and WTO *(World Trade Organization)*

> **Definition: "GATT was simply an independent multilateral treaty between member countries that laid down certain agreed rules for conducting international trade."**

GATT was formed, in the year 1947 with 23 countries as its founding members, including India for promoting international trade. Under GATT, EIGHT ROUNDS of negotiations took place between member countries, aimed at reducing tariff and non-tariff trade barriers in International Trade. These were :

1. Geneva, Switzerland (1947) - 7 Months
2. Annecy, France (1949) - 5 Months
3. Torquay, England (1951) - 8 Months
4. Geneva, Switzerland (1956) - 5 Months
5. Dillon Round, Geneva, Switzerland (1960-61) - 11 Months
6. Kennedy Round, Geneva, Switzerland (1964-67) - 37 Months
7. Tokyo, Japan (1973-79) - 74 Months
8. Uruguay, South America (1986-1993) - 87 Months

The eighth round referred to as the URUGUAY ROUND of multilateral trade negotiations, was the most complex and took SEVEN LONG YEARS to complete!

- The final act was signed at Marrakesh in Morocco on 15th April, 1994 and the agreement came into force on January 1, 1995. It marked the end of GATT and led to the birth of a new entity, the WORLD TRADE ORGANIZATION or WTO, as an independent body for overseeing international trade. Also, it was in the eighth round that for the FIRST TIME, GATT encompassed trade not only in goods but also in four new areas viz.
- Intellectual Property Rights (particularly patents in the area of plants and medicines)
- Trade in services (banking, insurance, mutual funds etc.).
- Textiles and clothing
- Agriculture

The final act strings together 25 agreements, declarations and decisions in the goods sector alone including Trade Related Aspects of Investment Measures (TRIMS), Trade Related aspects of Intellectual

Property Rights (TRIPS), General Agreement on Trade in Services (GATS) and the agreement on establishing the World Trade Organization (WTO).

Salient Features of new areas under the 8th GATT round

- **Agriculture**

  In the past, some countries did not apply rules of GATT to their own countries fully. They protected their inefficient and costly farm production by giving heavy subsidies, so that their products became 'artificially cheap' and depressed international prices. As a result, other countries did not get good prices for their produce. Also, they imposed quotas because of which entry of agricultural goods into their own country was controlled, but at same time their own produce was sold easily in international markets. However, under GATT these subsidies are reduced, so that fair play is ensured for all countries.

- **Textiles and Clothing**

  In the past, some countries enforced quotas on developing countries for this sector. Under GATT, these quotas are to be abolished over a ten year transition period which comes to an end on Jan 1, 2005.

- **Agreement on Trade Related aspects of Intellectual Property Rights (TRIPS)**

  Developed countries were unhappy trading with developing countries, because their goods and products got copied. They had to suffer huge losses in sales in the following sectors-pharmaceutical, chemical, movies and computer software. However, under WTO, protection for IPR on global basis has been ensured by bringing in uniformity of patent laws amongst member countries. Provision of exclusive marketing rights has been allowed, so that the original inventor gets rewarded. In India, the patent system did not allow protection of products in food, pharmaceutical, agricultural and chemical sectors and also biological material/plant varities. However, under TRIPS not only has India allowed patents in these segments, but duration of patent has also been increased from 14 years to 20 years.

- **General Agreement on Trade in Services (GATS)**

Trade in services is quite different from trade in goods. Industries producing goods are easily protected by imposing tariffs and cross-border restrictions. However, owing to the intangible nature of services, these measures become inapplicable in the case of services. GATS tries to overcome this by requiring member countries to modify their domestic rules and regulations, so that restrictions to services entering the country as well as those applicable to foreign service suppliers are eliminated. As part of its trade liberalization policy, India has already opened up its capital and technology services in the telecom, banking and insurance sectors. More than 150 service sub-sectors have been identified under GATS.

- **General Agreement on Trade Related Investment Measures (TRIMS)**

Countries often impose conditions on foreign investors to encourage the use of investment according to certain national priorities e.g Restricting Foreign Direct Investment in an Industrial concern to 49% so that govt. has major control. Such conditions are called Trade Related Investment Measures. Under GATT, countries are prohibited from using measures which are inconsistent with GATT rule of National Treatment and the rule which prohibits the application of quantitative restrictions to imported goods. TRIMS agreement applies to investment measures related to trade in goods only. According to it no country shall carry out any TRIM which is inconsistent with provisions of article III (relating to national treatment) or article XI (relating to quantitative restrictions) of GATT. It will allow countries to conduct trade throughout the world without any sector restrictions or control over how much equity is retained by a national of that country.

What led to formation of GATT?

- The need to rejuvenate industry
- The need to prevent polarization of countries

Industry was suffering badly after world war II, leading to recession in the world economy. The basic step to rejuvenate industry was to increase trade and this could only be done if different countries joined hands, so that market for goods became wide. Nations realized the benefits of "united we stand and divided we fall" especially regarding business and trade. Accordingly, different countries united to form trading BLOCKS. In fact, after world war II, the expression for trading blocs (blocks?) as NORTH OR WEST, EAST and SOUTH were quite often used to indicate the economies of various countries.

North or West refers to developed countries, South refers to developing countries and East refers to former socialist countries, most of which are in East Europe.

Based on friendly and trading relationships, a number of trading blocks came up in the world of trade e.g. EC (European community), EFTA (European Free Trade Association), NAFTA (North American Free Trade Agreement), OECS (Organization of Eastern Carribean States), ASEAN (Association of South East Asian Nations), SAPTA (South Asian Preferential Trading Agreement) etc.

Formation of an International Regime for trade was influenced after World War II, with the existence of three organizations viz.

- International Monetary Fund (IMF)
- International Bank for Reconstruction and Development (IBRD), popularly called 'World Bank'
- International Trade Organization (ITO).

The formation of ITO was recommended alongwith IMF and IBRD, in 1944 at the United Nations Monetary and Financial Conference, held at BRETTON WOODS, an area in the town of Caroll, New Hampshire (USA) to plan the future of an international monetary system. However, ITO never materialized.

Instead, as a result of the conference, the General Agreement on Tariffs and Trade (GATT) came into being in 1947. Hence, the system of IMF, IBRD and GATT is also known as the BRETTON WOODS SYSTEM.

GATT- OBJECTIVES

- **To prevent polarization of coutries and to provide due opportunities to underdeveloped and developing countries to participate in world trade**

  As trading blocks expand, there is an increased danger of polarization in the world-TRIPOLARIZATION. Greater Europe forming one pole, USA and South America forming second pole and finally Japan forming third pole. Danger of underdeveloped and developing countries in Africa and South Asia, including India being left out. From the point of view of global efficiency, the eventual objective was to have a global free trade that could not be fulfilled by trading blocs, because they represented bilateralism. What was needed for free trade was multilateralism, for which GATT was the answer.

- **To remove barriers to world trade**

  Under GATT, an attempt was made to remove barriers which hindered world trade namely Tariffs and Non-Tariff Barriers

(NTBs). Tariffs are basically custom duties, surcharge etc. . NTBs are restrictions on imports that do not work through prices, but through other means like quota or import license which are difficult to define, identify and quantify. GATT has had limited success in removal of NTBs but nonetheless has succeeded in enhancing world trade.

GATT Success!

- Increase in world trade- Over the period 1980-1992, world trade increased at an average annual rate of 3%.
- Benefits to Developing countries- Dollar value increased. Annual growth rate in terms of international trade for different countries :

Indonesia	–	7.3%,
China	-	8.7%
Thailand	-	10.3%
Chile	-	10.4%
Brazil	-	8.5%
Mexico	-	13.5%
Korea	-	23.5%
Hong Kong	-	13.5%
India	-	4.3%

Tariffs came down, but non-tariff barriers (NTB) continued to exist in the developed countries because of which developing countries competed for shrinking markets, undercutting prices and leading to slumps in exports. This is also called 'PREBISCH –SINGER' hypothesis according to which trade terms for developing countries will deteriorate in coming years. While exports could not be pushed up, imports of essential products could not be avoided e.g. petroleum products, capital goods, defence equipments etc. resulting in poor BOP (balance of payments) crisis in developing countries.

The Birth of WTO

WTO (World Trade Organization), based in Geneva, Switzerland is the successor to GATT. It was established on 1st January, 1995, under an agreement reached at the 8th GATT round of discussions held at Uruguay, 15th Dec. 1993 and the "Marrakesh Declaration", Morocco, 15th April, 1994. The WTO has 150 members, accounting for over 97% of world trade. Around 30 others are negotiating membership.

Purpose of setting up WTO

- To strengthen world economy,
- To increase trade and investment
- To promote employment and income growth globally.

WTO as of now has 150 members and India is one of the founding members of WTO.

Functions

- **Implementation of agreements:** WTO is responsible for admininistering and implementing multilateral and plurilateral trade agreements which together make up WTO.
- **Providing a Forum:** WTO provides a forum for trade related multilateral negotiations.
- **Policy making:** WTO co-operates with other international institutions involved in global policy making
- **Resolving of disputes:** WTO helps solve disputes between countries, pertaining to trade.
- **Monitoring:** Oversees national trade policies

Structure

WTO agreement contains 29 individual legal texts which cover everything from agriculture to textiles, from services to government procuremet, rules of origin and Intellectual Property. Added to these are more than 25 additional ministerial declarations, decisions and understandings which spell out further obligations and commitments for WTO members. Accordingly, structure of WTO has been organized to ensure efficient execution and implementation of various decisions.

- *Ministerial Conference*: Highest body of WTO. Composed of representatives of all members. Meets at least every two years and is empowered to take all decisions relating to multilateral trade agreements.
- *General Council (GC)*: Day to day functioning of WTO. Convenes in two forms
    - Dispute Settlement Body
    - Trade Policy Review Body

GC delegates responsibility to three other bodies (Councils fo Trade) viz.

- Councils for Trade in Goods
- Councils for Trade in Services
- Councils for Trade Related Aspects of Intellectual Property Rights

The Council for Trade in Goods oversees the implementation of agreements covering trade in goods, though many specific agreements have their own overseeing bodies. The latter two councils have responsibility for their respective WTO agreements and may establish their own subsidiary bodies if necessary. In addition there are various other committees and bodies.

Differences between GATT and WTO

1. **Institutional**: GATT was simply a set of rules and agreements followed by a group of countries, by mutual consent. It did not have any institutional foundation and had only a small associated secretariat which was established under the concept of International Trade Organization (ITO) in the 1940s. In contrast, WTO is a full-fledged body, having a permanent and well-established secretariat at Geneva.

2. **Permanency**: Even after 40 years of its establishment, GATT was still treated as something "provisional" and commitments made under it subject to revision and change. In contrast, WTO replaced GATT with full and permanent commitments.

3. **Focus**: GATT rules applied to trade in merchandise goods. However, WTO covers in addition to trade in goods, trade relating to Services and Intellectual Property also.

4. **Scope**: GATT was selective in execution of agreements and some of the agreements between members were restricted to select groups and were not applicable or acceptable to all. In contrast, agreements which constitute WTO are all multilateral and applicable to ALL MEMBERS.

5. **Dispute settlement**: Old GATT system was susceptible to blockages. In contrast, WTO dispute settlement system is faster, automatic and less prone to interference, as it enjoys more strengths and powers.

Though in name GATT has ceased to exist, yet its soul still lives on in the amended and updated version of GATT-1947 i.e. GATT-1994 is an integral part of the WTO agreement, and provides key guidelines to issues affecting international trade.

Important websites

1. **www.wto.org**

Official website of WTO. Gives very detailed information about WTO, history, future and current developments.

2. **http://www.globalexchange.org/campaigns/wto/**

This is an anti-WTO website, put up by activists who oppose WTO and its policies.

Address of WTO:

World Trade Organization,
rue de Lausanne 154, CH-1211
Geneva 21, Switzerland

7.2 DOHA DECLARATION

As discussed above, **GATT (General Agreement on Tariffs and Trade)** was a treaty between several countries. Its aim was to strengthen world economy and prevent world polarization by encouraging multilateral trade and removing tariff and non-tariff trade barriers. Since trade at a global level was being hindered because developed countries were reluctant to sell their products in countries where sufficient protection was not available to their products and these would be copied, under the 8th round of GATT, Intellectual Property Rights were brought within the scope of GATT.

This was carried out by the agreement on **Trade Related aspects of Intellectual Property Rights (TRIPS)**, under which rules for protection of intellectual property were made uniform in all countries which signed the TRIPS agreement, so that there was no fear in minds of member countries that their products would be copied in other countries.

Since rules for IP protection were governed by national laws, these could be changed only by legislation, which obviously was a difficult task for governments. Accordingly, **a ten year transition period** was allowed to all countries to make their laws compliant with TRIPS agreement. India too was a signatory to TRIPS and the ten year period ended on 1st January, 2005.

Background

A major cause of concern for developing countries was that in view of technological advantages of developed countries and protection offered under TRIPS, public health issues would be seriously affected as drugs would be monopolized and prices would rise. To address these concerns **DOHA declaration was signed** under which member countries were given the flexibility to overcome any problems relating to public health issues, which may arise as a result of TRIPS.

On one hand there was genuine concern that if a company has invested money and come up with an innovation, it should be rewarded by giving it monopoly through strong Intellectual Property Rights (Patents). On the other hand there was also concern that since most developing countries didn't have the same technological capacity as developed countries, their health systems would suffer because prices of drugs would rise. It was to address these concerns that DOHA declaration was signed.

What is DOHA* declaration?

" DOHA declaration is a legally binding agreement on all member countries which signed the TRIPS agreement, under which individual member countries have been given the flexibility to deal with problems relating to public health which may arise as a result of enforcement of TRIPS."

The **DOHA Declaration on TRIPS agreement and Public Health** was adopted by the WTO Ministerial Conference at Doha on 14th November, 2001 and consists of seven paragraphs **(Annexure-1)**.

History

The DOHA* declaration is the outcome of a process that started in early 2001 when upon the request of the African Group, the Council for TRIPS agreed to deal specifically with the relationship between the TRIPS Agreement and Public Health. The request of the African group was supported by other developing countries. It reflected growing concerns about the implications of the TRIPS Agreement (especially the provisions on patents) WITH REGARD TO ACCESS TO DRUGS.

* DOHA (pronounced "Ad dawhah") declaration is so called because it was signed in DOHA, main port and commercial center of Quatar. Quatar is a small Arabian country, situated just north of Saudi Arabia.

Initiating factors

It was the goal of TRIPS to foster harmony between different countries across the world by reducing tensions arising from imbalances in intellectual property protection. However intellectual property protection (patents) for pharmaceuticals AND ACCESS TO DRUGS IN PARTICULAR, remained a highly controversial issue. The following factors acted as catalysts in initiating the process which led to the DOHA declaration:

1. HIV crisis in sub-saharan African countries
2. Attempts by the pharmaceutical industry, backed by some governments to block the implementation of TRIPS-compatible measures by the South African Government
3. Complaint brought by the USA against Brazil in relation to compulsory licenses
4. Practical difficulties faced by authorities in developing countries in making use of 'flexibilities' provided in TRIPS agreement on issues pertaining to health.

These factors were manifestations of a conflict between the recognition of intellectual property rights (IPRs) and essential publich health objectives. In the TRIPS agreement itself, adequate flexibility had been provided w.r.t:

i. Exceptions to patent rights
ii. Parallel imports
iii. Compulsory licensing

However, when it came to practically making use of these 'flexibilities' authorities in the developing countries found that they faced considerable difficulties. Hence, members from developing countries wanted a specific declaration WHICH WAS LEGALLY BINDING and did not allow the TRIPS agreement to come in the way if members wanted to adopt measures TO ENSURE ACCESS TO MEDICINES and TO SATISFY OTHER PUBLIC HEALTH NEEDS.

Recognition of the need for conflict resolution

The need for resolving conflict between public health issues and TRIPS agreement had already been recognized by the WHO when it examined the relationship between public health and TRIPS in the World Health Assembly in 1996, in the form of a resolution on the REVISED DRUG STRATEGY. Subsequent resolution adopted by the World Health Assembly in 2001 addressed the need to evaluate the impact of the TRIPS agreement on access to drugs, local manufacturing capacity and the development of new drugs.

Events and important dates

June, 2001

- The Council for TRIPS systematically considered the relationship between public health and TRIPS for the first time in a special session in June, 2001.
- A number of developing countries, the European Commission and its Member States each submitted documents to the Council.
- Focus of the developing countries was to ensure that the TRIPS agreement did not undermine the legitimate right of WTO members to formulate their own public health policies as well as practical clarifications for provisions relating to:
    - compulsory licensing
    - parallel imports
    - production for export to a country with insufficient produc tion capacity
    - data protection

- The text also included a proposal for evaluation of the effects of the TRIPS agreement with particular emphasis on access to medicines and research activities pertaining to treatment of diseases mainly affecting developing and least developed countries.

- In response to the efforts made by developing countries, developed countries viz. USA, Japan, Switzerland, Australia and Canada circulated a non-paper with alternative text stressing the importance of IPP (Intellectual Property Protection) for research and development, arguing that IP (Intellectual Property) contributes to public health objectives globally.

- An EC non-paper was also circulated that proposed possible solutions to the problem of production for exports to fulfil a compulsory license in a country with no or insufficient production capacity.

August and September, 2001

- TRIPS Council held additional sessions to sort out the issue. Negotiations on these texts took place at General Council.

9-14th November, 2001

- WTO Ministerial Conference held at DOHA

- WTO members take the unprecedented step of adopting a special declaration on issues related to TRIPS and Public Health.

- Declaration signed by all members and adopted on 14th November, 2001 despite initial resistance by developed countries. Adopted by consensus on the basis of last minute compromises and a delicate balance in wording. While developing countries were essentially seeking a declaration recognizing their right to implement certain pro-competitive measures, notably COMPULSORY LICENSES and PARALLEL

IMPORTS as needed to enhance access to health care, developed countries did not view the TRIPS Agreement as representing a barrier to the achievement of public health objectives.

Salient features

1. The Declaration while acknowledging the role of Intellectual Property Protection for the development of new medicines, specifically recognizes concerns about the effect of such protection on prices of medicines.

2. It provides a legal right for members to take measures to protect public health and clearly states that 'the TRIPS agreement does not prevent members from taking measures to protect public health'.

3. It establishes a specific rule of interpretation that in event of any conflict/ambiguity regarding TRIPS, the deciding authority should opt for interpretations that are effectively 'supportive of WTO members' right to protect public health.'

4. The fact that the DOHA declaration provides flexibility at National level to member countries, has important political and legal implications. It means any pressures which are exerted by developed countries on others will run counter to the spirit and purpose of the agreement.

5. The declaration also provides flexibility to individual countries regarding public health crisis , which may represent ' a national emergency or other circumstances of extreme emergency' and that 'emergency may be a short-term or long-term situation.' In the event when action taken by one country is challenged by another country, the declaration places the burden on a complaining member country to prove that an emergency or urgency does not exist in the other country.

This represents an important difference with respect to earlier GATT/WTO jurisprudence which put the burden of proof on the member invoking an exception to its obligations. e.g. under TRIPS if India wanted to grant CL for a drug and USA complained, then India had to defend why it was granting a CL. However under the DOHA declaration, this has been reversed. If US complained, then it would have to prove that conditions for granting a CL e.g. emergency or urgency, did not exist in India.

6. A very important aspect of the declaration pertains to 'adoption of international principle of exhaustion of rights (determining the rules by which parallel imports may be accepted). The declaration provides freedom to member states to establish its own regime for such exhaustion WITHOUT CHALLENGE. (para 5 d).

   It is important to stress here that in order to take advantage of this and other flexibilities allowed by the TRIPS agreement and confirmed by the DOHA Declaration- national laws must incorporate the appropriate rules in the form of compulsory licenses, exceptions and other relevant provisions. Flexibilities do not automatically protect governments and private parties from legal action based on national laws, if these have not been modified. The effective implementation of the DOHA declaration in those countries therefore would call for an amendment to national laws so as to incorporate the exceptions and safeguards necessary to protect public health.

7. The DOHA declaration makes it very clear that DIFFERENTIATION IN PATENT RULES IS NECESSARY TO PROTECT PUBLICH HEALTH. The singling out of public health AND IN PARTICULAR PHARMACEUTICALS, as an issue needing special attention in TRIPS implementation constitutes recognition that public health related patents can be treated differently from other patents.

8. The DOHA declaration is a strong political statement that makes it easy for DEVELOPING COUNTRIES to adopt measures necessary to ensure access to health care WITHOUT THE FEAR OF BEING DRAGGED INTO A LEGAL BATTLE. The declaration

has got 'teeth'- it is not just an agreement. It is a Ministerial decision with legal effects on the Members and on the WTO bodies, particularly the Dispute Settlement Body and the Council for TRIPS.

9. Though access to medicines was the main preoccupation that led to the Doha Declaration, the Declaration covers not only medicines but any product, method or technology for health care. Thus the Declaration applies to pharmaceutical products, processes and uses, surgical, therapeutic and diagnostic methods, diagnostic kits as well as medical equipment.

10. While patents have been the focus of debate on the issue, the Declaration applies to all areas of intellectual property covered by the TRIPS Agreement, including protection of test data submitted for the marketing approval of pharmaceuticals (Para 1 of declaration—"public health problems....")

11. The declaration makes it very clear that the TRIPS agreement can be implemented in a manner supportive of WTO members right to protect public health. As a result, other members should restrain from any action that hinders the exercise of such rights by Members, especially developing countries and LDCs or Least Developed Countries (Para 4 of declaration).

12. The declaration specifically mentions that each member has the right to grant COMPULSORY LICENSES and the freedom to determine the grounds upon which such licenses are granted (Para 5 b). It is important to note that the expression 'compulsory license' is not found in the TRIPS agreement itself. The use of this terminology helps create awareness about this clause amongst developing countries/LDCs.

    Developing countries have identified compulsory licensing as one of the key instruments that may limit the exclusive rights of the patent owner when needed to fulfill certain objectives of public policy, particularly in order to ensure the availability of alternative sources for the supply of medicines at lower prices. Article 31 of the TRIPS agreement sets forth a number of conditions for granting of permission (compulsory licenses) viz. case-by-case determination, prior negotiation in certain cases with the patent owner, remuneration etc. but it DOES NOT limit the grounds on which such licenses are granted. Though Article 31 refers to some of the possible grounds (such as emergency and anti-competitive practices) for issuing compulsory licences, it leaves members full freedom to stipulate other grounds, such as NON-WORKING (of patents), public health or public interest.

Compulsory Licensing

"Compulsory license is a permission granted by the government in public interest, to a non-patentee to make a patented product".

It may be noted that in India, as per the provisions of Section 84 of Patents Act, 1970 and Clause 35 of Patents (Second Amendment) Bill, 1999, a compulsory license may be granted in case the patented invention has not met the reasonable requirement of the public at a reasonable price. This provision is intended to provide for necessary and adequate safeguard for the protection of public interest taking in to account the specific needs of a developing country like India.

Various grounds for this can be national emergency, epidemic, non-working of patent, high pricing of drug being imported etc. Under the Indian Patents Amendment Act, 2002 & Patents Rules, 2003 an additional ground for the grant of a Compulsory License has been inserted, viz. "the patented invention is not worked in the territory of India". An implication of this provision could be that the mere import of the patented product by the patentee in India may not be viewed as "working in the territory of India". The following grounds are also to be taken into account for grant of compulsory license:

- A circumstance of national emergency
- A circumstance of extreme urgency

- A case of public non-commercial use, which may arise or is required, as the case may be, including public health crises, relating to Acquired Immuno Deficiency Syndrome, Human immunodeficiency Virus, tuberculosis, malaria or other epidemics.

Some Pharma Multinational Companies (MNC's), bodies like Organisation of Pharmaceutical Producers of India (OPPI) had mooted introduction of a parameter for determination of the "reasonable price" regarding compulsory licenses, **('Patented Invention not available to the Public at a Reasonably Affordable Price' - is one of the grounds for the grant of compulsory licenses).** However, the Patent Rules, 2003 have not introduced any such parameters. In any event, the Rules cannot override or restrict the meaning of or operation of the main legislation.

The Government of India has also rejected a pharma MNC's proposition that the 'TRIPS agreement prohibits use of data filed in the course of obtaining regulatory clearance for commercial research' and has not included 'data exclusivity' in the Amendment Act, 2002.

Data Exclusivity

"Data exclusivity" is jargon for mandatory non-reliance on originator's data (mainly of drugs and agro chemicals), published to meet regulatory obligations , for unfair commercial use during a fixed period of time. In other words, the data filed by a company on the results of clinical trials and side effects should not be used by other companies for their commercial purposes.

Source: Patents Amendment Act, 2002 & Patents Rules, 2003
www.nishitdesai.com

A very good discussion on **DATA EXCLUSIVITY** is available at

http://www.southcentre.org/publications/protection/toc.htm

7.3 HATCH-WAXMAN ACT

As the world moves closer to the concept of a 'global village' by reduction and elimination of trade barriers, new challenges crop up. A case in point is the market for Generic Drugs (Drugs which are free from patent protection or not covered under patents). After facing a lot of protests and opposition on the homefront, India eventually signed the TRIPS (Trade Related Intellectual Property Rights) agreement under GATT (General Agreement on Tariffs and Trade) in 1995. Fears of increase in drug prices were brushed away as 'Myths and Misconceptions'.

It was felt that since 95% of the drugs being marketed in India were generics, introduction of a new IPR regime would not affect prices. Rather it was felt that the benefits were more-Indian Companies could license out new technologies and also tap global markets for their products. Indian Pharmaceutical companies enjoyed two 'homegrown'advantages viz. much cheaper manufacturing facilities and world-class medicinal chemistry skills, honed by years of reverse engineering.

However, what is the reality? Can Indian Companies really tap overseas markets, for new Drug Discoveries or Generic Drugs? Are generics also under some form of Intellectual Property Protection? A clear understanding of the protective mechanisms for generics is the key to successful exploitation of overseas markets.

For pharma students and researchers, understanding the IPR issues involved in case of Generic Drugs is very important as a significant chunk of the pharma industry is engaged in the manufacture of generic drugs.

The Hatch-Waxman Act

(Also known as the Drug Price Competition and Patent Term Restoration Act)

"The Hatch-Waxman Act is an act dealing with the approval of generic drugs and associated conditions for getting their approval from the Food and Drug Administration (FDA), market exclusivity, rights of exclusivity, patent term extension and Orange Book Listing."

The act was enacted in the USA in 1984. It is in force in the United States only and not in India. It was necessitated by the following observations:

- **Absence of Generic drug manufacturing:** Sometime in the year 1962 it was observed in the USA that out of the 150 off patent drugs in the market, there were no generic drugs! Owing to cumbersome approval procedures, manufacturers were simply not interested to take up manufacture of generic drugs, even though these were cheaper.
- **Cumbersome regulatory procedures:** Many companies did not go in for manufacture of generic drugs because of the impractical and non-scientific manner in which the regulatory authorities viewed the approval process and insisted upon proving the obvious.
- **Patients were denied the option of cheaper drugs:** Owing to the cumbersome procedures involved, drug companies did not want to waste time and money on clinical trials of generic drugs, insisted upon by regulatory authorities. This resulted in denial of the option of cheaper drugs to patients.

The Hatch-Waxman Act addressed these issues and proposed many reforms, **including the mechanism for approval of generic drugs**, which had to be initiated as **Abbreviated New Drug Application (ANDA)**, for the purpose of market approval.

Purpose of the Act

- **Promotion of generic drug manufacturing:** The act aims at promoting generics without putting them through the tough and long approval process involving clinical trials etc. so that the medicine prices burden on patients can be reduced.
- **Encouraging competition as a tool for checking drug prices:** The underlying objective of the Act is that in the absence of generic drugs, it is difficult to check the profiteering motive of the patent owner of a drug, who may put patients to ransom! However, at the same time it also takes care of the interest of the patent owner and provides relief for undue lengthy process.

> It is important to note that the Act does not consider making or using a patented invention an act of infringement, if it is used only for development and submission of information under a Federal Law which regulates the manufacture, use or sale of drugs. Hence, there is no restriction on when R&D on a generic drug should start.

General Provisions of the Act

1. **Maintaining list of patents which would be infringed**: Each holder of an abbreviated new drug application (ANDA) must list pertinent patents it believes would be infringed if a generic drug were marketed before expiration of these patents. The FDA maintains a list of such patents in its publication, Approved Drug Products with Therapeutic Equivalence Evaluations (commonly known as Orange Book).
2. **Only Bioavailability studies and not clinical trials needed for approval**: FDA can only ask for bioavailability studies in respect

of an ANDA and not for clinical trials etc. (For bioavailability FDA uses the ± 20% test i.e. the amount of active ingredient in the blood serum over a period of time has to come within ± 20% of that which is observed with the patented drug)

3. **Para I, II, III and IV certifications**: While filing an ANDA, a generic firm must certify any one of the following:

   I. Patent information on the drug has not been filed (in the orange book)

   II. Patent has already expired

   III. Date on which patent will expire, and that the generic drug will not go to the market until that date passes

   IV. Patent is invalid and will not be infringed by the manufac ture, use or sale of the generic drug

The above certifications are also called Para I, II, III and IV certifications. In case of certification I and II, approval for manufacture can be granted immediately. In case of III, approval for ANDA can be made effective from the date of patent expiration. In case of IV, it is mandatory for the manufacturer to notify the original patent holder, **who can take upto 45 days** to bring an infringement suit against the manufacturer, if he feels his IPRs are being violated. However, if no such action is taken within the stipulated period, certification of the ANDA applicant will be accepted by the FDA.

If an infringement action is brought in time, FDA must suspend approval of the ANDA until the date of court's decision. If the court decision goes in favour of the patent owner, FDA will suspend the approval till expiry of the patent. FDA does not wait indefinitely- the maximum time available for coming to a decision is 30 months (2.5 years) after the expiry of 45 days i.e. filing of a reply by a drug manufacturer within 45 days will result in delay of a minimum of 2.5 years for the generic drug maker!

The first generic applicant to file paragraph IV certification is awarded a 180 days (6 months) market exclusivity period by the FDA. The six month exclusivity period will start at the earliest of the two dates- the date of commencement of commercial marketing of the generics or the day a court decides that the patent which is the subject matter of para IV certification, is invalid or not infringed.

4. **Data exclusivity period for NMEs**: New Molecular Entities approved by the FDA will enjoy data exclusivity for a period of 5 years from the date of approval of the NME by the FDA. A generic version cannot be approved during these five years.

5. **Data exclusivity period for supplements**: Supplements requiring clinical trials will enjoy 3 year data exclusivity period.

6. **Extension of the original patent term**: Original patent term can be extended by a maximum of five years, if undue delays take place during the regulatory process (FDA approval).

Recent Changes to the Hatch-Waxman Act

Under the Medicare Prescription Drug and Modernization Act of 2003, some changes have been made in the existing Hatch-Waxman Act as follows:

1. **Non-extension of the 30-month period**: As per modified rules, only one 30 month stay will be permitted in case of those patents listed in the Orange Book, when an ANDA is filed under paragraph IV certification. Modifications to the 30 month stay are allowed based on district court judgements. Patent holders included new patents in the Orange Book after receiving notification regarding para IV certification and thus extended the 30 month period.

2. **Time limit for informing patent owner** : The company filing ANDA under para IV must submit full and complete information over and above what is necessary under current law and must notify the patent owner within 20 days.

3. **Provision for allowing declaratory judgement**: If patent owner does not file infringement proceeding within 45 days of notification issued by ANDA applicant, the applicant may request for a declaratory judgement and thus avoid being sued. If sued, applicant may file a counter claim requiring patent owner to make changes in the orange book listing. This favours the patent holder, because he does not have to pay any damages for not modifying the Orange Book listing in time and there is apparently no time limit for making such modifications.

4. **Benefit of exclusivity for several ANDAs filed on same day allowed**: It is now possible for many generic companies to qualify for the 180 day market exclusivity if several ANDAs are filed on the same day.

Implications of the Act for manufacturers of generic drugs

- **Monopoly extension beyond patent term:** Under the Hatch-Waxman Act, the government has a system of patent term 'restorations' under which monopoly of the original patentee can be extended for a maximum period of 5 years in addition to the initial patent term. In the European Union also there exists a system of supplementary protection.

- **Reward for pediatric trials:** As of 1997, the US allows a six-month exclusivity period as a reward for studying the drugs in children. Also, US allows as a reward 6 months exclusivity period to the first generic manufacturer to file a successful para IV certification alleging that a patent is invalid or not infringed. Thus, as far as the export of generics is concerned, it faces important IPR hurdles today in the markets of EU and the US.

How IPRs are used by patent holders to block entry of generic drug makers?

Though generics offer cheaper alternatives to existing, branded drugs, it is not a cakewalk for the pharma companies. It is true that the generics market is largely risk free, but the generics segment not only faces IP related challenges but market challenges too. Paragraph IV filings are generally accompanied by intense and expensive litigation against big pharma companies. Challenging patents and associated legal costs can be quite high. Sometimes litigations can run into US $15-18 million to be successful. Also, there is intense competition from the market.

1. **Use of legislative provisions and loopholes to apply for patent extension.**

   As of now, 5 year period is already allowed to condone for delay in approval.

2. **Suing generic manufacturers for patent infringement**

   Being aware that their drug cannot come off patent when there is ongoing patent litigation, the original patent holder files suits against generic manufacturing claiming infringement on one or more layers of patents subsequently filed on various, and often insignificant elements of the drug. To date such cases are going on in the US for Claritin, Cardizem, Buspar and Prozac. Under the Uruguay Round Restoration Act (URRA) the US provided an extension of three years as gratis extension. This way Zentac of Glaxo gained an additional nineteen months of protection. Claritin got an extra 22 months of exclusivity. Claritin was able to extend its patent life further by six months for an estimated $ 3 million pediatric trial, but for the company (Schering-plough) the gain made through this alone was $ 1 billion. Estimates exist that through these and other legal tricks total gains for Claritin have been of the order of extra four and half years of patent life which may give additional $13 billion to Schering-plough.

3. **Merging with direct competitors to retain monopolies**

   Rather than allow generic drug makers to enter the market resulting in fall in prices and loss of profits, companies prefer to merge with competitors to maintain monopolies and thus profits.

4. Recombining drugs in different ways to claim new patents

Simply by recombining drugs or using other 'tricks' sometimes companies are able to get patents, which block the entry of generic drug makers. Similar trick was used by Europe's biggest drug maker, GlaxoSmithKline for its highest selling asthma drug Seretide also called ADVAIR having global sales of US $2.2 billion . Patent granted to GSK's was challenged by the generic drug makers on grounds of obviousness. The case was fought in the London High Court. The main grounds on which the patent rested was whether an inventive step was involved in combining two older drugs, Flovent and Serevant to make Advair. Justice Pumfray of the London High Court ruled that the combination was entirely obvious and cancelled the patent. The victory for generic drug makers meant that they could launch cheaper versions of the inhaled asthma treatment as early as October, 2005.

Recombining drugs in slightly different ways to secure new patents is a real cause of concern for a country like India where the local industry has capabilities to provide competition to global pharmaceutical industry. According to the Report of the National Institute of Healthcare and Medicines (NIHCM), between 1989 and 2000 incrementally modified drugs (IMDs) constituted 54% of all drugs patented and approved by the FDA in the USA.

Examples

1. Benefits of ANDA filing to get six months exclusivity

- In August 2001, Dr.Reddy's Labs (DRL) won a 180- day exclusivity for Fluoxetine which netted the company $70 million in six months.

- When Ciprofloxacin went generic, 10 players including DRL launched their version of the drug on day one. This was UNPRECEDENTED and prices collapsed by 95%.

CASE STUDIES — Innovators Vs Generic Drug Makers

Case 1 Pfizer vs Dr.Reddy's Labs (DRL)

In February, 1986 Pfizer was granted a patent on a class of compounds that treats heart disease and hypertension. The patent covered the molecule amlodipine, including two of its salts- amlodipine besylate and amlodipine maleate. In 1987, Pfizer filed another application for amlodipine besylate salt specifically, as studies conducted showed it was superior in treating hypertension, and marketed it as Norvasc. As the patent's expiry date approached (25th Feb, 2006), Pfizer went ahead and filed a Patent Term Extension (PTE) under the Hatch-Waxman extension rules.

Meanwhile, in 2002 DRL tried to get approval for manufacture of AmVaz under the generics category in view of the significant returns estimated at $200 million over a three year period. DRL filed an abbreviated new drug application (ANDA) for same under USFDAs 505(b) 2, seeking marketing approval after it was found the PTE by Pfizer was only for amlodipine besylate. On 31st October, 2002 USFDA granted approval to DRL to go ahead. However, Pfizer sued DRL for **patent infringement**, insisting that PTE covered the entire scope of amlodipine. Pfizer lost the case in a New Jersey district court in Dec.2002 but won the same in a higher court in Feb.2004, thus putting an end to DRL attempts to tap a lucrative market in the generics segment.

The IPR issues in this case touch several facets:

1. **Extension of IPP**: Even after expiry of patents, IP protection can be extended to compensate for the loss to the innovator during the approval process. Presently, this extension period is restricted

to five years. Pfizer was able to get IP protection for its drug amlodipine besylate (Norvasc) even after expiry of the patent.

2. **Broad nature of IP coverage**: The basic patent coverage is quite broad and a generic drug maker may find it tough to manufacture even the generic versions after expiry of the patent term. DRL was not granted permission to manufacture amlodipine besylate (AmVaz) even though the Drug had not been covered under the PTE. DRL followed necessary legal procedures and even won in a lower court, but ultimately did not get permission.

3. **IPR issues extend to generics also**: DRL simply wanted to make a drug whose patent term had expired and which the original patent company had not marketed at all. Still it was unable to get permission.

4. **Ethical issues-** A pharmaceutical giant, Pfizer is already actively making profits on one version of the drug. It has not undertaken production of the other version, even after 20 years. When it seeks extension, it does so for only the version it has marketed (Norvasc). Yet when another company in the US wants to manufacture the version which has neither been marketed nor applied for under patent extension (AmVaz), Pfizer puts in all out effort to block the same. It loses once. Does not give up. Fights in a higher court and wins the case. Is it ethically correct on part of the company? What in your opinion are the points in favour of Pfizer? After all it did win the case in a higher court.

Case 2 Pfizer vs Ranbaxy Labs

In Jan, 1983, Pfizer was granted a patent for its anti-fungal drug Diflucan. When Ranbaxy initiated the process for launch of a generic version of the drug, it was sued by Pfizer on grounds of patent infringement. Pfizer also sought PTE for six months for a pediatric version of the drug. The infringement suit against Ranbaxy was terminated on Jan 29, 2003 when the original term of the patent came to an end. However, Pfizer was granted an extension of six months till July, 29, 2003 during which Ranbaxy could not launch the generic version.

PS: Diflucan which treats fungal infections, had sales of US $ 1.2 MILLION in 2003.

Case 3 Aventis SA and Albany Molecular Research vs

DRL and others

Five companies which sought to market generic versions of Allegra antiallergy pill were sued by the parent company for infringement of its patents which expire in 2013. Dr.Reddy's Labs (India), Barr Pharmaceuticals, Mylan Pharmaceuticals, Impax Laboratories of US and Israel's Teva Pharmaceuticals were all sued by Aventis SA, France's biggest Drug Maker and partner Albany Molecular Research. Production of generics were halted.

Case 4 GlaxoSmithKline vs Cipla Ltd., IVAX (USA) and two other generic firms

The case pertained to Europe's biggest Drug Maker, GlaxoSmithKline. Patent granted to GSK's biggest selling asthma drug Seretide also called ADVAIR having global sales of US $2.2 billion was challenged by the generic drug makers on grounds of obviousness. The case was fought in the London High Court.

The main grounds on which the patent rested was whether an inventive step was involved in combining two older drugs, Flovent and Serevant to make Advair. Justice Pumfray of the London High Court ruled that the combination was entirely obvious and cancelled the patent. The victory for generic drug makers meant that they could launch cheaper versions of the inhaled asthma treatment as early as October, 2005.

Case 5 UCB vs DRL

Dr.Reddy's Labs has been sued by Belgian Pharma major, UCB for patent infringement. DRL had filed ANDA with the USFDA for Levetiracetam tablets (250, 500 and 750 mg). Levetiracetam is the generic version of UCBs Keppra TM, for which patent rights are held by UCB. It is used for the treatment of epilepsy. The brand has annual sales of US$ 234 million.

CASE STUDIES — Compulsory Licensing

Case 1: Compulsory License granted to Cipla for anti-retroviral (HIV-AIDS) formulations

Cipla became the **first company in the world** to benefit from the issuance of compulsory license (CL) for import of drugs issued after 30th August, 2003 WTO decision to allow flexibilities in the patent laws to deal with health emergencies. The CL was issued by the Malaysian Govt. to a national firm, Syarikat Megah Pharma Vaccines, to import specified anti-retroviral patented drugs in different doses from CIPLA. These drugs are Didanosine and Zidorudine. The patent for the first drug is held by Bristol Myer Squibb and the other drug is held by GSK. The drugs have to be supplied to government hospitals in Malaysia for a period of two years.

Case 2: Issue of Compulsory License (CL) by Kenyan Govt. for manufacture of anti-pneumonia drug

The Kenyan Govt. has initiated a process to issue a compulsory license to procure antibiotic AZITHROMYCIN, a new generation drug for which Pfizer Incorporation holds patent rights. Indian drug companies who manufacture and market the drug include Wockhardt, Alembic and FDC. The license issued by the Kenyan Govt. would expect the CL holder to produce azithromycin formulations in quanties that are enough to treat over two million cases of pneumonia in Sub-Saharan Africa. Market of the drug which is marketed by Pfizer under the brand name ZITHROMAX is close to US$ 1 BILLION.

Case Study of an Indian IP SAVVY Company- ORCHID Chemicals and Pharmaceuticals Limited (www.orchidpharma.com)

Orchid Chemicals & Pharmaceuticals Ltd. is a global pharmaceutical company headquartered in Chennai, India. It is involved in the manufacturing and export of cephalosporin and non-cephalosporin bulk actives, formulations and nutraceuticals. It is India's largest manufacturer and exporter of cephalosporins and is the first company in India to pioneer 'zero discharge manufacturing process'. It is an excellent example of a company voluntarily promoting eco-ethics.

Over the last few years, it has filed over 150 patent applications, which is about four times the number of applications filed by the company during the initial three years of its intellectual property rights (IPR) activity.

The company has institutionalized its IP processes by setting up an exclusive IP department to nurture creativity and innovation in its R&D team.

CASE STUDY — Pirating of Indian Drug by a US company

Herbal drug 'Jeevani' developed by Tropical Botanical Garden and Research Institute (TBGRI) with the traditional knowledge supplied by the Kani tribals, was registered by the New York based NutriScience Innovations LLC, as a 'fatigue busting wonder drug' under the US trademark rules, without TBGRI'S knowledge. The drug was patented in India by TBGRI in 1996 and subsequently the manufacturing and marketing rights sold to Coimbatore Arya Vaidya Pharmacy for seven years.

The patent violation came to light when TBGRI was preparing to float an international tender for the sale and manufacture of the drug after the expiry of its existing agreement with the Coimbatore company.

Some definitions of Generic Drugs on the Web

- A prescription drug, which is chemically equivalent to a brand-name product, dispensed under its generic chemical name. (benefitsu.stanford.edu/glossary/glossary.html)
- Drugs marketed under their nonproprietary name rather than a brand name. (www.hsl.unc.edu/lm/druginformation/glossary.htm)
- A prescription drug that has the same active-ingredient formula as a brand-name drug. A generic drug is known only by its formula name and its formula is available to any pharmaceutical company. Generic drugs are rated by the Food and Drug Administration (FDA) to be as safe and as effective as brand name drugs and are typically less costly because advertising costs are not included. (www.cwru.edu/med/epidbio/mphp439/Dictonary.htm)
- Copies of innovative products sold by multiple manufacturers once any limited market exclusivity period has expired. (*www.canadapharma.org/Patient_Pathways/Glossary_Terms/*)
- Less expensive drugs, but of the same therapeutic value. Generic medicines appear on the market when the protection of original leading medicines, assured by a patent, is expired. (*www.euromut.be/uk/lexique.htm*)

Important site for information on Orange Book

www.fda.gov/cder/ob/default.htm

Practice Questions:

1. Are patents the sole factors which determine drug prices?
2. Express your views on whether fears about shooting drug prices due to strong patent laws are correct or not.
3. Do you think a 'world patent' will be useful? Why? What are the positive and negative aspects of the same?
4. Present case studies on patents and drug prices with respect to ARV drugs.
5. Which are the main organizations at international level whose policies should be aware of as a pharma professional, especially in the context of drug prices and availability?
6. What were the benefits of GATT? Why did it come to an end if it was so successful?
7. Express your views on whether the Pharma Industry in a country stands to gain or lose if that country becomes a member of the WTO?
8. Does Biotechnology related IPR have any relevance for Pharma sector? How?
9. Knowledge and technical skills are key assets for a successful business. Can knowledge, innovations and IP skills help us in competing in global markets? Why? How?
10. What were the ethical issues involved in GSKs Advair drug? How come a patent got granted in the first place? Should the company be made to pay for the exclusivity it enjoyed for so many years? Elaborate reasons for your reasons.

11. With reference to the cardiovascular drug case of Pfizer vs DRL, what were the legal and ethical aspects of the IPR issues involved? What in your opinion would have been ethically correct?

12. With reference to Pfizer Vs Ranbaxy in the Diflucan Case, what were the fundamental IPR issues involved? Ranbaxy would be able to manufacture the drug after six months anyway. Do you think denial of permission for six months to a generic drug maker matters? How?

13. Explain compulsory licensing and data exclusivity. Do they have same meaning or are they different?

Annexure- 1

Doha Declaration on the TRIPS Agreement and Public Health

WORLD TRADE ORGANIZATION

WT/MIN(01)/DEC/W/2 14 November 2001

(01-5770)

MINISTERIAL CONFERENCE

Fourth Session

Doha, 9 -14 November 2001

DECLARATION ON THE TRIPS AGREEMENT AND PUBLIC HEALTH

Adopted on 14 November 2001

1. We recognize the gravity of the public health problems afflicting many developing and least-developed countries, especially those resulting from HIV/AIDS, tuberculosis, malaria and other epidemics.

2. We stress the need for the WTO Agreement on Trade-Related Aspects of Intellectual Property Rights (TRIPS Agreement) to be part of the wider national and international action to address these problems.

3. We recognize that intellectual property protection is important for the development of new medicines. We also recognize the concerns about its effects on prices.

4. We agree that the TRIPS Agreement does not and should not prevent Members from taking measures to protect public health. Accordingly, while reiterating our commitment to the

TRIPS Agreement, we affirm that the Agreement can and should be interpreted and implemented in a manner supportive of WTO Members' right to protect public health and, in articular, to promote access to medicines for all.

In this connection, we reaffirm the right of WTO Members to use, to the full, the provisions in the TRIPS Agreement, which provide flexibility for this purpose.

5. Accordingly and in the light of paragraph 4 above, while maintaining our commitments in the TRIPS Agreement, we recognize that these flexibilities include:

   (a) In applying the customary rules of interpretation of public international law, each provision of the TRIPS Agreement shall be read in the light of the object and purpose of the Agreement as expressed, in particular, in its objectives and principles.

   (b) Each Member has the right to grant compulsory licences and the freedom to determine the grounds upon which such licences are granted.

   (c) Each Member has the right to determine what constitutes a national emergency or other circumstances of extreme urgency, it being understood that public health crises, including those relating to HIV/A1DS, tuberculosis, malaria and other epidemics, can represent a national emergency or other circumstances of extreme urgency.

   (d) The effect of the provisions in the TRIPS Agreement that are relevant to the exhaustion of intellectual property rights is to leave each Member free to establish its own regime for such exhaustion without challenge, subject to the MFN and national treatment provisions of Articles 3 and 4.

6. We recognize that WTO Members with insufficient or no manufacturing capacities in the pharmaceutical sector could face difficulties in making effective use of compulsory licensing under the TRIPS Agreement. We instruct the Council for TRIPS to find an expeditious solution to this problem and to report to the General Council before the end of 2002.

7. We reaffirm the commitment of developed-country Members to provide incentives to their enterprises and institutions to promote and encourage technology transfer to least-developed country Members pursuant to Article 66.2. We also agree that the least-developed country Members will not be obliged, with respect to pharmaceutical products, to implement or apply Sections 5 and 7 of Part II of the TRIPS Agreement or to enforce rights provided for under these Sections until 1 January 2016, without prejudice to the right of least-developed country Members to seek other extensions of the transition periods as provided for in Article 66.1 of the TRIPS Agreement. We instruct the Council for TRIPS to take the necessary action lo give effect to this pursuant to Article 66.1 of the TRIPS Agreement.

CHAPTER-8

What are the career options for me in the area of IPRs?

For a student, the first and foremost question regarding any new study area or subject is 'how useful will this be for me in getting a job?' As IPRs are yet to be introduced in professional colleges, but expectations of knowledge of IPRs is there during interviews, this handbook can be very useful. In this chapter, career options for pharma professionals in the area of IPRs are discussed. Job profiles and expected skill sets, apart from technical background are also discussed.

8. What are the career options for me in the area of IPRs?

To enable students to read this chapter independently, the basic concepts and questions on IPRs have been addressed again in a simplified and concise manner.

1. What are Intellectual Property Rights?

These are legal rights which are granted for creations of the mind. Just as you have rights over your car, house etc. (property) because you have paid for it and have valid documents to prove it, so also in case of IPRs. If you have created something e.g. a song, poem or a book or even a new invention which has commercial application or value, you are entitled to get 'rights' for it.

2. Why is the word 'Property' used in case of Intellectual Property?

Intelletual Property or 'creations of mind or intellect' are like 'property' ie. have commercial value. They can be bought and sold just like conventional property e.g. a house or a car. Example: If Lata Mangeshkar has sung a song and a company wants to make cassettes of it for sale, the company pays money to the singer to get the rights. In other words, the song becomes an "Intellectual Property" for the singer. Similarly, if a biotechnologist has developed a new process for making an enzyme, it has lot of commercial value for a company making that enzyme. The biotechnologist will first have to create rights over his work e.g. by filing a patent. Then he can sell it to the company. Since, IPRs can be bought and sold just like property, we use the terms 'intellectual property'.

3. What is the need for IPRs?

Intellectual Property Rights are needed to reward original effort. The fundamental concept behind all forms of IP be it patents or copyright or industrial design etc. is that the person who has put in original effort must have rights over his creation and must get reward for it. He must not be cheated. Example: as cited above, if a biotechnologist has developed a new process for making an enzyme, having lot of commercial value for a company making that enzyme, he can get paid for his effort e.g. through cashdown payments or royalties. He is thus stimulated to go in for more innovations. However, if his efforts just get copied, he may not put much effort again for more innovations and developments. Thus, IPRs lead to progress and development by ensuring rights and recognition for people who put in original effort.

4. Don't IPRs hinder research? Will it not be good for society if there are no IP barriers and one is free to use knowledge

Regarding hindrance to research, IPRs promote research rather than hindering it. Patent databases disseminate the latest technical information free of cost, so that researchers can avoid duplication of work, identify hot areas of commercial interest and also avoid infringing upon somebody else's rights.

IPRs are not barriers to research- nothing prevents researchers from using information in patents for further research. Also, patents are valid only in the country where they are filed. Researchers in other countries can freely use these patents, even for commercial purposes, legally and without any hindrance. On the other hand, if there were no IPRs how will you protect the researcher who has put in original effort? e.g. if a scientist has worked on a project and come up with a breakthrough technology and it just gets copied. Will he be motivated? No. It is very important to protect the rights of people who put in original effort and hard work. That is why IPRs are needed.

5. How as a pharma student/researcher, IPRs are important for me?

As mentioned above, IPRs are of different types. The category of IPR most important for researchers is patents. Knowledge of IPRs (Patents) is important for graduates, not only if they want to pursue higher studies but also if they want to get placements. In case of higher studies, involving research, knowledge of IPRs can be useful for researchers as follows:

- **Prevents duplication of work**: Search of patent databases reveals what has already been done before, thus saving precious time and money. Quite often, industry may just file patent for an innovation, and not publish it.
- **Helps researchers to focus on commercially relevant research**: Patents are for work having commercial value. For researchers formulating research projects, a review of patent databases quickly reveals what is 'hot' and what is not!
- **Prevents exploitation of workers**: By enabling researchers to have 'legal rights' over their work, IPRs prevent exploitation of workers and ensure proper remuneration, in case their work is used for commercial purposes.
- **Helps in revenue generation**: Licensing of patents helps to earn money – for researchers and also the institute and departments. This in turn leads to financial freedom- better research facilities, scholarships, improved infrastructure.
- **Important source of technical information**: Patents are the ONLY source regarding detailed technical information, which is unlikely to be available anywhere else. While number of journals may be in hundreds, the patent database per country is only one, making consultation much easier.
- **Prevents infringements and helps avoid litigation**: A basic knowledge of IPRs enables researchers to respect others rights and decide whether their work is infringing or not, especially in commercial segment.

- **Stimulates creativity**: By enabling researchers to see at a glance the level of technological achievement in a particular field, patents stimulate creativity. They impose challenges as to how to take achievements even further.

6. What are the advantages of being a patent agent?

A patent agent is a technically qualified professional who has been duly authorized by the patent office of a country, to deal with patent related matters. Different countries have different procedures for registering a patent agent. In India, the basic requirement if a person wants to become a patent agent is to qualify a written examination conducted by the patent office. Details for the same are available at www.ipindia.nic.in. For pharma graduates, advantages of being a patent agent are as follows:

- **Broader career opportunities**: With R&D companies, consultancy firms, patent attorneys
- **Thorough knowledge of patenting procedures in India**: Theoritical concepts become clear, enabling you to not only file patents for your own inventions, but also to help your colleagues or other inventors who may not have the specialized knowledge which you have.
- **License to practice**: As a qualified patent agent, you are duly authorized to file patents for others and also to defend the same in front of the controller. Your science background alongwith knowledge of IPRs gives you an edge over others, who may be having only technical knowledge but not that of IPRs.
- **Flexibility to operate:** Your office is in your 'head'- you don't need very large infrastructure e.g. labs, workshops etc. for this type of work. All you need is a fast internet connection and knowledge of IPRs coupled with a science background. This gives you tremendous opportunities to operate anywhere, which is a very important factor for qualified female professionals.

- **BPO opportunities:** Business Process Outsourcing is becoming popular and for a qualified patent agent, significant work can be sourced on the internet, if one puts in effort.

7. Do I need a legal background for making use of IPRs?

No. Just as you don't have to be a mechanical engineer to drive a car, so also for making use (driving?) IPRs you don't have to be a legal expert!

What is required is a technical background, which you already have. Just as in driving a car, you pick up the fundamentals- steering wheel, clutch, brake; so also in IPRs what you need are fundamentals- whether the work you are doing is really original? Is it infringing upon somebody's rights or not? What is the global technology status of the research work you are about to start? Whether what you have achieved in the lab is patentable or not? What are the basic requirements for filing a patent? and so on...... For all this, you really don't need a legal background. Yes, you might seek the 'assistance' of lawyers and legal experts, in case you are filing a very important patent. Lawyers in IPR are quite often people with technical backgrounds with a degree in law. They can help you in 'polishing' your patent, making it difficult for anybody to copy or break it easily. It is always a good idea to seek professional help, but it is not wise to 'block' any initiative on your part for knowing about IPRs just because you don't have a legal background.

8. What are the career opportunities for me if as a researcher in pharamaceutical sciences, if I also polish my IPR skills?

Knowledge of IPRs is critical for industries as well as teaching institutes, in the pharmaceuticals sector. It is also very important in case you are going in for higher education. The planning of your research project, its success and ultimately acceptance by industry - all depends upon your knowledge of IPRs.

Regarding career opportunities:

- First and foremost candidates having a working knowledge of IPRs e.g. even those who have completed basic courses of WIPO get preference during interviews and placements.
- Secondly, your placement opportunities get broadened. Candidates with a technical background alongwith IPR qualifications are also sought after by patent attorney firms and also leading consultancy firms in addition to Industry. IPRs are a part of every industry affecting a wide variety of segments- R&D, Production, Marketing, Strategic Planning etc.
- Lastly, more and more institutes are introducing IPRs as a subject and openings at faculty level in these areas are growing.

9. What will be my job profile, if as a researcher I also acquire IPR qualifications?

Firstly, as mentioned above candidates with IPR qualifications over and above their technical qualifications are likely to get faster placements and also better pay packages in any industry they join. Since industries are gradually realizing the immense importance of IPRs in enhancing business profits, IPR cells are being created in Industry. Professionals with IPR skills stand to join these departments and have stronger chances of promotions as compared to conventional departments in which manpower is readily available.

So, your first and foremost job profile can be joining the IPR Department in a pharmaceutical industry. Your job profile/activities are likely to be as follows:

- networking with R&D people and finding out what they are doing
- determining whether any of their work is patentable

- identifying technological advances of relevance to your industry vide regular monitoring and search of patent databases
- guiding your R&D colleagues to avoid any research work which is infringing and go in for work which is free from infringements,
- identification of new and emerging technologies which can benefit your industry and so on.

You must now be realizing, that IPRs rely heavily on technical skills which YOU ALREADY HAVE. Legal skills are needed for filing of patents, infringement cases etc. for which services of qualified professionals can always be hired. However, the amount of work required in the background BEFORE you actually seek the services of a patent attorney is considerable and that is where you are needed.

Secondly, you can also be hired directly by an attorney firm. Filing of patents requires a sound technical knowledge and most firms are happy hiring M.Sc/ M.Pharm/ Ph.D candidates. Legal and related skills will be gradually built up once you join a firm and start working.

Thirdly, you also have career opportunities in leading consulting firms. Lastly, IPR strong candidates always have good opportunities abroad- it is a niche area, in which trained human resources are not that readily available!

10. How are IPRs and technology management linked? Are there any career opportunities for me in technology management? I am a science professional and have no background in technology management- can I still enter the area of technology management?
IPRs and technology management are like the two wheels of a bicycle- both are important! Patents filed but not commercialized are a tremendous loss of time, money and effort. Hence, their commercialization aspects are also important. Filing a patent is in fact the FIRST STEP in technology management. Once rights over the work are created, inventors can freely contact and interact with

industry professionals, disclosing details of their work without any fear that their work will be copied.

Regarding career opportunities in technology management, there is a lot of demand abroad for technology professionals.

In fact almost every university in Europe and the United States of America, has an office of technology transfer and licensing. Hence, there is a demand for technically qualified people who can work in this area.

It doesn't matter if you are just a science professional because that is a fundamental requirement. However, it is important that you do an MBA after your M.Sc. or Ph.D. A degree in law after Ph.D. is also a very good combination for technology professionals. By now you must have realized the power of 'hybrid degrees' e.g. M.Sc./M.Pharm. followed by MBA or LLB or Ph.D with LLB, for technology professionals. It is a different career but being different is what results in faster promotions and better packages! If you are doing whatever everybody else is, don't expect higher salaries or faster promotions!

Reprint of an article " CAREERS IN TECHNOLOGY TRANSFER" is given at the end of this chapter which is quite informative.

11. Where can I learn more about technology management?

Two very good and informative sites for the same are **www.apctt.org** and **www.autm.org.** Both are very well-designed and easy to browse sites. Visit them- they will be quite an eye-opener for you!!

12. At our institute, IPRs and Technology management as a subject is yet to be introduced in the syllabus. Can any help be provided?

This guidebook has been written in a manner, to facilitate the introduction of a 'IPR teaching program' in any pharmaceutical institute. A proposed syllabus has also been provided as a guide to potential teachers. The chapters have been written in the form of lectures and due coverage has been given to all aspects in a manner, that students of pharmaceutical sciences can understand and make practical use of the power of IPRs. It can be for improving the quality of their research work and also making their work benefit society. However, in case any additional help is required, author may be contacted at pbansal.niper@gmail.com

Concluding remarks

IPRs and Technology management- these are two 'golden keys' which result in the practical application of research. Research is carried out for the progress and benefit of society and is funded largely by the hard-earned taxpayers' money. Ensuring its practical application is thus a very important area- an area which opens up new career opportunities for pharma professionals.

***

The Scientist 2000, 14(17):32
4 September 2000

Careers in Technology Transfer

"Field offers 'terrific' job opportunities, but practical experience is essential"

by Karen Young Kreeger

Ever since the Bayh-Dole Act of 1980, which allows universities, federally funded research labs, and small businesses to own and patent inventions discovered in federally funded research programs, the profession of commercializing research has been growing and changing. Technology transfer managers help shepherd an idea conceived by scientists in academia or government research centers to commercialization in the private sector. They deal with evaluating discoveries for commercial potential, patenting and licensing commercial rights, and brokering deals with potential investors. Professionals in this area are employed at universities, medical centers, federal research labs, and in industry.

The job market right now for scientists or anyone with the right experience and credentials to enter technology transfer is "terrific," says James Severson, president of the Association of University Technology Managers (AUTM) and president of the Cornell Research Foundation, the technology transfer unit for Cornell University in Ithaca, N.Y. "I think this reflects the growing need to have qualified people in these offices and ... the job market in the country in general."

There are 2,300 members in AUTM, with 90 percent from the United States and Canada. Every member has some technical background, from B.S. to Ph.D. degrees. But Severson says that he couldn't even guess how many hold Ph.D.s or other advanced degrees. AUTM plans to do a demographic study of its membership sometime next year. The Licensing Executive Society (LES) is another professional organization for tech transfer professionals. Of its 5,000 members, about one-third are associated with some aspect of health care.

According to Severson, a current general job description for a position in technology transfer might read: "Experience in business with a minimum of a B.S. in a scientific discipline needed. Advanced degree--J.D., MBA, or Ph.D.–preferred."

A Job Seeker's Market

Federal labs such as the National Institutes of Health, private companies, and universities and medical centers are all vying for qualified candidates for their growing tech transfer offices. "Right now I have five positions open in my office," says Maria Freire, director of NIH's Office of Technology Transfer. "It's a very competitive market as far as hiring is concerned." For these and most other positions, she notes that training in life sciences is necessary. After that an MBA, J.D., or some kind of comparable business experience is needed. Freire and others also look for creativity, flexibility, the ability to recognize a good idea, and knowledge of how to craft a deal and move it forward. She adds, though, that for NIH the primary goal is not to maximize revenue, but to guide NIH research into the hands of the public.

There's a two-pronged structure of tech transfer at NIH: the central office that Freire heads and a technology development coordinator at each institute. The NIH office also sponsors unpaid summer internships that are often filled by Ph.D.s, MBAs, and J.D.s, but the spots are highly competitive.

Tech transfer in the private sector approaches new innovations from the other side of the commercialization coin. Randolph J. Guschl, director of the Center for Collaborative Research and Education at DuPont Co. in Wilmington, Del., relates that his center looks for joint development projects with university researchers. "My role is as a liaison between DuPont and scientists in other sectors." Guschl has a Ph.D. in chemistry and was an R&D director for 12 years before moving into tech transfer seven years ago.

He notes that candidates for tech transfer positions are a bit younger than they were when the field started. "It's only been in the late 1980s to early 1990s that industry offices have come about to work with government and academic scientists," says Guschl. "Now more and more young people right out of business or law school with a technical background are stepping immediately into centers like mine, whereas before they needed to have some kind of managerial experience."

He says that qualified students and postdocs can get relevant business experience profiling companies and mining the technology literature for potential ideas to commercialize, especially in university offices. The experiences to assemble, says Guschl, are a mix of business knowledge to recognize the value of technology and negotiate a deal; legal knowledge for contracts; and a technical background to evaluate the potential of a discovery.

In an academic-based tech transfer office, Todd Sherer, director of the Technology and Research Collaboration Office at the Oregon Health Sciences University (OHSU) in Portland, typically becomes aware of discoveries when principal investigators from his institution call to tell him about their latest research. Or, especially in the biomedical field, he hears from a company that already is aware of OHSU research from attending scientific meeting presentations. From there, he and his staff follow up with investigators, determine the marketability of the research, discuss the research program's experiment and publication schedule, go over the patenting and intellectual property protection process with the researcher, and ultimately find a commercialization partner.

The OHSU tech transfer office employs three Ph.D. scientists--one chemist and two life scientists--as licensing officers, although, adds Sherer, a Ph.D. is not required for these positions. He says that he constantly gets graduate students and postdocs looking to gain experience in his office, but timing is key. He only takes on people when an extra pair of hands is needed. Sherer himself has a Ph.D. in molecular biology and has worked the last 10 years in tech transfer. "Ten years ago if a person just had a Ph.D. and no business background it was easier to break into the field," he recalls. "Now the field has evolved so much that people have the interdisciplinary experience, but job seekers can pretty much write their own ticket" if they're mobile, flexible, and have the right training and experience.

That Old Conundrum: Experience

But how can a postdoc, graduate student, or more established scientist gain the necessary business experience? Although there are no formal degrees in technology transfer, many professionals suggest paid or unpaid internships in tech transfer offices. "It's very rare that an office will hire someone with no business experience," says Severson. "It's obligatory to even get your resume considered."

Other avenues for experience include MBA courses that encompass evaluating scientific projects for commercial potential or taking AUTM or LES courses, schedules of which are listed on their Web sites. Some scientists are advisers to patent law offices and gain experience that way. When it comes to the job hunt, positions are listed also on the AUTM and LES Web sites and sometimes in the Wall Street Journal, the Chronicle of Higher Education, and the classified sections of local newspapers.

The National Technology Transfer Center (NTTC), which links U.S. companies with federal research labs, also sponsors training courses and apprenticeships. Paula Clemons, an NTTC marketing administrator, says that over 4,000 people from companies, federal labs, and universities have attended its various courses, which run from a couple of days to two weeks. They teach the basics of technology management as well as more advanced subjects such as licensing, marketing, and technology evaluation. The courses are held on site, at companies, and sometimes in larger urban areas like New York City and Washington, D.C. Clemons isn't sure how many people with science backgrounds take the courses with a career in tech transfer in mind but mentions that training would be beneficial for scientists looking to get practical experience.

NTTC also runs the Entrepreneurial Technology Apprenticeship Program (ETAP), whose purpose is to recruit students from historically black colleges and universities and other minority institutions like tribal colleges for nine-month internships in technology management. These cooperative positions are located predominantly at federal research labs such as Sandia National Laboratory and NASA. The scientific subjects that they learn to manage vary, but can include life sciences. Most ETAP students have just completed undergraduate programs or are graduate students and come from both science and business majors. In the last five years 40 students have completed the program, states Franz Alcindor, ETAP administrator.

Over the last five years, the qualifications to enter technology transfer have become more specific, notes Severson, partly because the field is evolving and the skills needed are becoming more specialized. "The best advice I can give someone thinking about entering technology transfer is that practical experience is invaluable for your resume," he concludes.

- Karen Young Kreeger (kykreeger@aol.com) is a contributing editor for The Scientist and author of Guide to Nontraditional Careers in Science (Philadelphia, Taylor & Francis, 1999).

CHAPTER-9

How can I improve my qualifications in the area of IPRs?

In this chapter, addresses of universities, list of IPR courses being offered, fee structure, qualifications etc. are provided so that students who want to work further in the area of IPRs can easily pursue these. Emphasis is given on distance learning courses, so that a student while pursuing his main degree is able to polish his skills in the area of IPRs also!

9. How can I improve my qualifications in the area of IPRs?

Simple! Make a beginning by joining free courses conducted by the World Intellectual Property Organization, Switzerland!

Founded in 1974, WIPO is a specialized agency of the United Nations. Details of the free courses are available at **http://academy.wipo.int**

DL-001: This is an intellectual property primer course of JUST THREE HOURS which you can easily complete online after registering free. It consists of 12 sections followed by a series of self-assessment questions.

DL-101: This course (General Course on Intellectual Property) is comparatively more advanced, requiring about 50 hours of study over a six week period. It includes audio segments, self-assessment questions and also multiple-choice, end of module tests. It is an excellent course for building IPR basics. The notes can be downloaded once you register and there is an online test at the end of the course. The test is of 'open book' type ie. conceptual type in which one has to apply the knowledge and concepts given in the notes. A certificate is sent to all the qualifying candidates, from WIPO Switzerland, at the end of the course, free of cost.

Other useful free resources of IPR information: These can easily be located by using 'google' 'altavista' or any other suitable search engines and typing 'IPRs' or 'Intellectual Property Rights' and 'teaching courses'. A good site is www.patentmatics.org. The govt. site on patent related information e.g. **www.ipindia.nic.in** is quite informative.

Distance Learning Courses in IPRs by Indian Universities Post-graduate Diploma in Intellectual Property Rights (one year) : IPR distance learning courses are offered by the following:

- National Law School of India University (NLSIU), Bangalore **(http://www.nls.ac.in)**
- NALSAR University, Hyderabad **(http://www.nalsarlawuniv.ac.in/)**
- University of Mumbai, Mumbai **(http://www.mu.ac.in/fc_law.html)**
- IGNOU: Indira Gandhi National Open University **(www.ignou.ac.in/schools/sos/courses.htm)** also offers a one year course entitled "Graduate Diploma in Intellectal Property Rights (PGDIPR)".
- University of Hyderabad offers a P.G.Diploma in Cyber Laws &Intellectual Property Rights (PGDCL & IPR) of one year duration. **(http://www.uohyd.ernet.in/cdenew3)**
- Industry Program in Drug Design and Patenting - 1 year offered by **Bioinformatics Institute of India (BII), Noida (www.bii.in)**
- Industry Program in Intellectual Property Rights- 1 year offered by **Bioinformatics Institute of India (BII), Noida (www.bii.in)**
- PG Diploma in Intellectual Property Rights- 1 year offered by **Bioinformatics Institute of India (BII), Noida (www.bii.in)**

Certificate Course on Intellectual Property Rights

- Indian Law Institute, New Delhi (deemed university) **(http://www.ilidelhi.org/e-learn.htm)**

International Courses in IPRs (LLM) for Pharma Researchers (ONE YEAR DURATION)

The courses offered by various universities and institutes abroad in the area of IPRs can be easily located by respective students, on the internet. Some well-known institutes in the area are:

1. **Franklin Pierce Law Center, New Hampshire, USA (http://www.piercelaw.edu)**

   Programs offered (http://www.piercelaw.edu/ipb/ipbaf.htm)

   Master of Laws in Intellectual Property,Commerce and Tech nology (LL.M.)

   - Master of Intellectual Property, Commerce and Technology (MIP/CT)
   - Diploma in Intellectual Property

Fee and other expenses

Tuition for the 2006–2007 school year (August–July) is $30,550 (or Rs. 13. 6 lacs approximately). Living expenses are estimated at $16,863.00 (or Rs. 7. 5 lacs approximately) ie. a total estimated budget of Rs. 21 lacs approximately for Indian Students.

The **Franklin Pierce Law Center** (Pierce Law or FPLC) is a private, American Bar Association approved law school, located in Concord, New Hampshire. The school is named after the 14th President of the United States and New Hampshire native Franklin Pierce and is the only law school in New Hampshire.

The school holds an annual Intellectual Property Summer Institute in cooperation with Tsinghua University Law School in Beijing. In addition, Pierce Law offers students the opportunity to study in Ireland at the eLaw Summer Institute, a collaborative effort between Pierce Law and the University College Cork Faculty of Law.

The school is highly recognized for its Master of Laws in Intellectual Property, Commerce and Technology. It is also the only law school offering a graduate degree in intellectual property designed for scientists, engineers and any interested persons not holding a law degree (M.I.P.).

Ranking:

Pierce Law's IPR program has consistently ranked among the top ten law schools in the U.S.

2. University of Turin, Italy (www.turin-ip.com)

- **Master's of Law in Intellectual Property (LLM)**

The Master of Laws in Intellectual Property is organised by the University of Turin Law School and by the World Intellectual Property Organization Academy, Switzerland in cooperation with the International Training Centre of the International Labour Organization (ITC-ILO) in Turin.

An interesting (and very useful aspect!) of the LLM program of the University of Turin is that of the total duration of 12 months, 8 months is in DISTANCE LEARNING MODE. Students are required to put in only 4 months at Italy, which makes the program highly affordable. Tuition fee is Euro 7500 or approximately Rs. 4,38, 000/- (excluding govt. taxes on fee and boarding and lodging).

Concluding Remarks

For students desirous of polishing their qualifications, distances learning courses in IPRs are a powerful tool. It is strongly recommended that pharma students and researchers put their knowledge of IPRs to good practical use in terms of improving research quality and planning.

Annexure

How to use this Handbook as an IPR teaching manual?

A basic IPR syllabus is proposed below, to facilitate the teaching of IPRs at Graduate/Post-graduate level, by existing faculty. The total duration of a lecture is presumed to be 1 hour, in which the teacher would be using modern teaching aids e.g. LCD projector, OHP slides etc. to cut-down the teaching time.

To cover the entire syllabus, 20 teaching sessions may normally be required, which generally equals a 1 credit course i.e., 1 hour per week, which most research institutes and universities should be able to introduce easily in their course curriculum.

Caution! Only the basic concepts should be discussed, to ensure easy understanding of the topic and also stimulate interest of the students. Remaining details can be easily 'absorbed' by the students from the guidebook, once the basics are clear.

Some useful tips for teachers

Teaching IPRs can be quite a challenge, owing to its unique 'dry nature' ! Some tips to create and hold the interest of students are as follows:

1. Procure and distribute actual copy of a patent (You can easily download one from www.uspot.gov). You may have problem viewing figures-don't get discouraged. All it needs is a bit of free software (tiff) which has to be downloaded. The patent site provides necessary directions.
2. Collect actual products from market, which have IPR in them e.g. a product bearing a patent number (a children's pencil in which lead points can be used by pushing in from the top is a patented item). Similarly, some chinese or imported items will have words 'patent pending' or 'patented' written on them. Once you start looking around, you will be surprised by number of

'IPR' related products you come across- medicines, cosmetics and consumables e.g., talcum powders, shaving creams, patented having razors etc.

3. Involve the students, give them practical assignments etc. If possible, organize a visit to the national patent office.
4. As far as possible, make the teaching sessions interactive, focussing on practical aspects. Invite IPR experts from industry, other institutes.

PROPOSED BASIC IPR SYLLABUS

FOR INTRODUCTION AT GRADUATE/POST-GRADUATE/Ph.D LEVEL, FOR PHARMA STUDENTS

(20 lectures or 1 credit course/per semester) spread over 5 modules. 2 examinations included- mid-term and final).

Module 1	**5 lectures**	Introduction to Intellectual Property Concepts
Module 2	**5 lectures**	Practical aspects of patenting. Mid-term exam.
Module 3	**4 lectures**	Making research benefit society
Module 4	**3 lectures**	Important IPR related treaties and international agreements.
Module 5	**3 lectures**	Career options in IPRs. Final exam.

Annexure

How to use this handbook as an IPR teaching manual for Pharma students/researchers?

An important aspect of this handbook is that owing to coverage of a very broad range of IPR aspects and concepts, it can be easily used as a 'teaching manual' also. It represents a 'single window' source of information, thus facilitating taking of lectures on IPRs by existing faculty. Introduction and teaching of IPRs, thus practically becomes easy.

Annexure

How to use this Handbook as an IPR teaching manual for Pharma students/researchers?

A basic IPR syllabus is proposed below, to facilitate the teaching of IPRs at Graduate/Post-graduate level, by existing faculty. The total duration of a lecture is presumed to be 1 hour, in which the teacher would be using modern teaching aids e.g. LCD projector, OHP slides etc. to cut-down the teaching time.

To cover the entire syllabus, 20 teaching sessions may normally be required, which generally equals a 1 credit course ie. 1 hour per week, which most research institutes and universities should be able to introduce easily in their course curriculum.

Caution! Only the basic concepts should be discussed, to ensure easy understanding of the topic and also stimulate interest of the students. Remaining details can be easily 'absorbed' by the students from the guidebook, once the basics are clear.

Some useful tips for teachers

Teaching IPRs can be quite a challenge, owing to its unique 'dry nature' ! Some tips to create and hold the interest of students are as follows:

1. Procure and distribute actual copy of a patent (You can easily download one from www.uspot.gov). You may have problem viewing figures-don't get discouraged. All it needs is a bit of free software (tiff) which has to be downloaded. The patent site provides necessary directions.

2. Collect actual products from market, which have IPR in them e.g. a product bearing a patent number (a children's pencil in which lead points can be used by pushing in from the top is a patented item). Similarly, some chinese or imported items will

have words 'patent pending' or 'patented' written on them. Once you start looking around, you will be surprised by number of 'IPR' related products you come across- medicines, cosmetics and consumables e.g. talcum powders, shaving creams, patented having razors etc.

3. Involve the students, give them practical assignments etc. If possible, organize a visit to the national patent office.

4. As far as possible, make the teaching sessions interactive, focussing on practical aspects. Invite IPR experts from industry, other institutes.

PROPOSED BASIC IPR SYLLABUS

FOR INTRODUCTION AT GRADUATE/POST-GRADUATE/Ph.D LEVEL, FOR PHARMA STUDENTS

(20 lectures or 1 credit course/per semester) spread over 5 modules. 2 examinations included- mid-term and final).

Module 1	5 lectures	Introduction to Intellectual Property Concepts
Module 2	5 lectures	Practical aspects of patenting. Mid-term exam.
Module 3	4 lectures	Making research benefit society
Module 4	3 lectures	Important IPR related treaties and international agreements.
Module 5	3 lectures	Career options in IPRs. Final exam.

Total - 20 lectures/sessions (inclusive of two examinations)

MODULE -1 INTELLECTUAL PROPERTY CONCEPTS

Number of Lectures: 5

Contents

Chapter 1: What are IPRs?

- **Lecture-I:** Concept of Property, conventional property vs intellectual property, similarities and differences, Importance of Intellectual property rights, different mechanisms for IPR protection- need and types.
- **Lecture-II:** Basic aspects of the 8 different IPR mechanisms viz. patents, copyright, trademark, industrial designs, layout designs of integrated circuits, geographical indicators, plant varieties and trade secrets.
- **Lecture-III:** IPR vs Regulatory.

Chapter 2: How are IPRs practically useful for pharma students and researchers?

- **Lecture-IV:** Role of intellectual property rights in research. How pharma students can practically utilize the power and benefit of IPRs to improve the quality of their research work.
- **Lecture-V:** Various factors affecting choice of IP protection- whether patent is the only form of IP suitable for researchers or there are other forms too? When to file and not file a patent?

MODULE -2 PRACTICAL ASPECTS OF PATENTING

Number of Lectures: 5

Contents

Chapter 3: How can I file a patent?

- **Lecture-I:** Patentable and non-patentable inventions. Essential criteria for filing a patent. Filing patent in India- appropriate forms, their format , fee and time lines. Mode of submission and frequently asked questions.
- **Lecture-II:** Drafting of patent application.
- **Lecture-III:** International patenting- Regional routes and national routes. PCT/WIPO. Regional offices. Possibility of world patent.
- **Lecture-IV:** Recent amendments in the Indian Patent Act and its significance for Pharma Professionals.Basic concept of mailbox applications or WTO applications.
- **Lecture-V: Mid-term examination**

MODULE -3 MAKING RESEARCH BENEFIT SOCIETY

Number of Lectures: 4

Contents

Chapter 4 : How should I commercialize my patent?

- **Lecture-I:** Need for commercialization of research. Role of IPRs in research commercialization. Introduction to TOT and COT concepts (transfer of technology and capture of technology).
- **Lecture-II:** Drafting of technology offers. Strategic planning for research commercialization- as individual and with help of organizations. Leading organizations at national and international level helping in commercialization of research.

Chapter 5 : How can I integrate IPRs into my research work?

- **Lecture-III:** Integration of IPRs into research- interlinking research with patents. Strategies for avoiding research duplication, infringements. Using patent databases as tools for identifying buyers of research/future employers.

Chapter 6: Why are ethics important in the study of IPRs?

- **Lecture-IV:** Ethics and their significance for professionals. Factors affecting ethics. IPRs and ethics- why? Case studies.

MODULE - 4: IMPORTANT IPR RELATED TREATIES AND INTERNATIONAL AGREEMENTS

Number of Lectures: 3

Contents

Chapter 7 : What are the important IPR related treaties and international agreements I should be aware of as a Pharma student?

- **Lecture-I:** Concept behind GATT- why it came into existence? Trade related Intellectual Property Rights (TRIPS) and related agreements (TRIMS/GATS). Factors leading to end of GATT and formation of WTO (world trade organization). Strucuture of WTO. Differences between GATT and WTO. Present status and challenges.
- **Lecture-II:** DOHA declaration: Reasons for the declaration. Implications of the clauses.
- **Lecture-III:** Hatch -Waxman Act: IPR issues concerning generic drugs. Para 1, 2, 3 and 4 filings. Case studies.

MODULE - 5: CAREER OPTIONS IN IPRs

Number of Lectures: 3

Contents

Chapter 8: What are the career options for me in the area of IPRs?

- **Lecture-I:** Career options in the area of IPRs for Pharma students. Job profiles and expected skill-sets.

Chapter 9: How can I improve my qualifications in the area of IPRs?

- **Lecture-II:** Introduction to WIPO distance learning courses. Courses offered by Indian Universities in area of IPRs. Reputed international institutes. Degrees offered in area of IPRs.

  Duration and fee schedules.

- **Lecture-III:** Final examination

Total lectures = 20

NOTES

NOTES

NOTES

NOTES

www.ingramcontent.com/pod-product-compliance
Lightning Source LLC
Chambersburg PA
CBHW071331230926
51849CB00002B/366
9789352300181